Holy Ways
of Wales

of Pentecost in Ghana. This work was started just fifty years ago by Irishman James McKeown, whose story has been recorded by Christine Leonard in her book *A Giant in Ghana* (New Wine Press). James and his wife Sophia sang and danced their way into Ghanaian hearts and today there are 4,000 churches, with hundreds in neighbouring countries. This single denomination is growing at the rate of five new churches every week. What's more, they don't consider a group with less than fifty adults qualifies as a church!

While in Jerusalem in May 1989 I sat at table with a mild-mannered, rather quiet African brother who I later learned was William Kumuyi from Nigeria. 'What do you do?' I enquired. 'I'm a pastor,' he replied. Endeavouring to keep the conversation alive I asked him 'how many people he had in his church.' He paused and thought for a moment. I suspected he was doing a finger count under the table. 'Fifty thousand,' he eventually revealed with no more enthusiasm than I would have showed if I had said '200'. I quickly asked another question before he could turn the conversation around and ask me about my church.

What he didn't tell me was that his church had also planted 1,000 other churches throughout Nigeria and the countries close by. The last I heard was that the main church had reached 65,000 and is now the fifth largest church in the world.

According to the 1989 Lausanne II official statistics, number one is Yoida Full Gospel Church, Korea, with 700,000; two is Jotabeche, Chile, with 350,000; three is Vision of the Future, Argentina, with 145,000; four is Brazil for Christ, Brazil, with 80,000 and five is William Kumuyi's church, Deeper Life, Nigeria, with its 65,000 members. Furthermore, the top 10 largest churches in the world are all either charismatic or Pentecostal, and it is estimated that soon the largest 100 will all be charismatic or Pentecostal too! No one can afford to ignore these figures; they surely give testimony to what the Holy Spirit can accomplish when he is given freedom to move in his own way.

Preceded by the Spirit

Early in 1990, Christine and I found ourselves in a remote part of the Transkei, one of the South African homelands, in a little village, with no amenities and mostly mud huts, called Lujizweni, in the Ngqeleni district – actually we couldn't find the name on a map. We were ushered into the newly erected church building to find a packed congregation worshipping and praising God in typical African style. Joseph Kobo, the leader, had been what some would call an ANC terrorist. Almost twenty years of his life had been spent in and out of prison, including eighteen months in solitary confinement on the infamous Robben Island. There he finally came back to the Lord.

Behind him, on the platform, was a chalkboard which proudly announced 'Our goal for this decade of evangelism – ten new churches every year.' It was then half way through February. 'How's it going?' Ken Rose, my travelling companion, asked at the close of the service. 'We've planted three new churches in six weeks, so we are ahead of our schedule,' we were told, as though this kind of growth was the norm. 'Where did you hear about the decade of evangelism?' Ken pressed them further, wondering if their inspiration had come from Lausanne II or some other well known initiative. 'The Lord spoke to us about it. Why, are there other Christians with a similar vision?' they enquired. Later, we spent an hour hearing from Muriel, an excited lady leader, how God had spoken to them prior to our ministry concerning many parallel truths and revelations. We could hardly believe it. The Holy Spirit had been there before us; our job was simply to confirm what he had already shown these people. By May of the same year four more churches had been planted, bringing the total to seven, and leaving them a full seven months to reach their target.

But what of Asia? Until recently I thought that everyone had heard about the tremendous happenings in Korea, where almost 30 per cent of the whole nation have turned to acknowledge Jesus as Lord in a few decades. However, when I asked our friends in the Transkei where the world's largest church was, they had absolutely no idea. I don't think they had ever heard of Korea, let alone Seoul or Yonggi Cho! It is just that the same Spirit is at work in both places. How thrilled they were as I went on to tell them about Dr Kriengsak Chareonwongsak's work in Thailand. In less than 10 years, God has used him to raise up a church of 6,000 in the city of Bangkok, mainly of men and women converted directly from Buddhism. In addition, over 70 new churches have been established and recently 1,000 young people gave themselves to serve in church planting throughout the whole country.

We also told them of the time spent with Paul Raj, a Lutheran friend, who works in Bhadrachalam, southern India. After spending four years getting to know the people of an unreached tribal grouping, with no written language, Paul began walking the villages singing, testifying and talking about Jesus. Today, almost 20 years on, he bears the scars of persecution on his body but there are now churches in most of the 250 villages he considers to be in his parish, with over 18,000 converts baptised and going on with God. They still have no Bible in their own tongue. What a privilege it was for Christine and me to live with these wonderful people in their lathe-and-mud homes, teaching them and praying with them and their families.

Then there are the Anglicans in Singapore under the leadership of Bishop Moses Tay and men like Canon James Wang. Because of their devotion and stand on the baptism in the Holy Spirit, they have virtually been labelled a cult by some of their own brethren. But God continues to bless them. Now around 12 per cent of that island nation confesses Christ.

I could go on to talk about Central and Latin America where, in some countries, God has raised up men, unknown to us, who have preached to larger meetings and seen greater numbers of converts than Billy Graham himself. Recently, I listened to Lynn Green, UK director of YWAM, who reported that Chile, for example, is almost 25 per cent Christian now and Guatemala has very nearly reached the 50 per cent Christian mark! Of course not all of these are charismatic or Pentecostal, but many are. Some Roman Catholic groups have experienced renewal, which is seen in thriving communities and prayer groups of many thousands strong. In certain previously unreached areas, jungle tribes are hearing the gospel and turning to Christ as a result of dedicated, long-term efforts by single-minded missionaries. What's more, many of the new churches in these nations are catching the vision of evangelisation and sending out missionaries all over the world, including to Europe, the cradle of so many movements and so much of the church's history.

Expansion in Europe

However, even here in Europe, now said to be the darkest continent, there is a stirring, with Roman Catholics at the forefront in some countries. For example, the little island of Malta, with its population of 300,000, has around 10,000 Holy Spirit-filled Catholics, many of whom are young in years and the faith but on fire for

God. Great conferences, inspired worship and training is giving way to evangelistic zeal as bands of young people are being sent out to all areas of the world. France and Italy also have similar Catholic initiatives, with large and growing communities springing up. But they are not alone. Englishman Phillip Wiles, who has been living in Sicily for years, and working with local evangelical Pentecostal leaders, is seeing a number of independent churches established, in Sicily and on the mainland, the largest of which is approximately 800.

In Portugal, too, there are huge charismatic churches of up to 7,000, with hundreds being converted every month. One Pentecostal group, called Remar, working mainly with drug addicts throughout Spain, is seeing evangelistic communities established in many places. I asked Miguel Diez, one of the leaders, 'Do you have any ex-addicts in the leadership of your communities?' Without hesitation he replied, 'Yes, 300!'

Worldwide renewal

Yet, with all of these random headlines from my own experiences and contacts, I'm hardly scratching the surface of what is going on among God's people worldwide. I haven't mentioned Hong Kong and the tremendous work of Jackie Pullinger among the addicts of the Walled City; or Norway where, in some areas, there's a new awakening, primarily among traditional Christians, which some are calling revival; or Australia, with its fast growing, huge Pentecostal churches; or the multiplicity of islands scattered throughout the oceans of the world where God is at work – I hear of some which boast 90 per cent Christian populations.

I've not considered North America, where, in spite of setbacks resulting from the over-publicised misdemeanours of some telly evangelists, the church of

Jesus is doing 'pretty good, thank you very much', and we can praise God for the work of men such as Jack Hayford, Larry Lea and John Wimber among many, many others. I've said nothing about Eastern Europe, where, from country after country, reports are filtering through of amazing blessings and developments in the churches. May God continue to pour out his Spirit upon them and may we, lovingly, stand with them during this new phase of freedom and, hopefully, increased prosperity. May they not fall foul of the snare of materialism which has hindered the churches of Western Europe. I've not touched on the vast, unreached areas of the world which, in the past, we have reckoned to be the Enemy's strongholds. The Middle East, Turkey, Albania, North Africa and even Israel (picked at random) are just a few of the 'impenetrable' locations from which are coming exciting vibrations and rumblings – a new church here, 1,000 Muslims come to Christ there, secret evangelism elsewhere. And so it goes on and on....

The UK too is experiencing blessing. In spite of major decline across the denominations between 1,500 and 2,000 new churches with up to 200,000 attending, have been established in the last couple of decades. That's a bright spot on what's been a pretty dark horizon. These statistics may seem doubtful, but I was recently at a conference of leaders from new churches. Fifteen networks attended representing approximately 1,000 churches, one or two of which top the 1,000 mark in their congregations. Add to these the networks not represented and the non-aligned churches and you'll see my estimates are not far out. There are also now fresh winds of renewal blowing through many traditional, historic and independent churches. The effects of this are seen in the ever growing numbers at Spring Harvest, events like the March for Jesus and the prayer concerts and summer Bible conferences which are being arranged nationwide. Bible training courses and colleges are filling up, and large numbers are getting involved in mission teams and evangelism at home and overseas.

Preparation for battle?

All in all, although we dare not be complacent, we have very much to give thanks for. The Lord has slowly but surely been softening the hard hearts of we Christians. He has poured out his Spirit without regard to our defences. In crossing the traditional barriers which have kept Christians apart for centuries, the Lord has clearly shown himself to be Head of the church. He has surprised us again and again, just as he did in New Testament times by baptising in the Holy Spirit those who were considered to be outside the circle of his purposes or the sphere of his blessing. He has declared his intent to work with and through all those who acknowledge him to be the King of kings and Lord of lords. We would be foolish to ignore this amazing phenomenon of charismatic renewal, this almost universal rain of Pentecostal blessing. Surely, we must question why we are receiving such an outpouring at this precise point in history. Jesus never did anything without a purpose. He has always had some objective and those who are closest to him will understand his heart and his goals.

Could it be that all this is preparation for a last great onslaught on the very 'gates of hell', in order to release the multitudes who are held in the grip of sin, false religion and demonic forces? Could it be that our generation is being made ready for the final and greatest battle of all: Armageddon – the conflict which will bring an end to the evil world system and its injustices, making way for the kingdom in all its fullness; a battle in which the church, having played her part in the preparations, will look on as Christ makes the overwhelming victory he accomplished on the cross a visible reality? Whatever we believe about the immediacy of these events, we should live as though they were the truth and channel all our energy and efforts towards achieving this goal in our lifetime. For if the Holy Spirit's activity in the church indicates an imminent tidal wave of God's judgement and blessing, what else should our response be?

Jesus, when speaking of his midnight-hour return, (Mt 25:1–13), indicated where we are most likely to fail. The ten virgins he referred to all had invitations to the wedding, they were all called to be light-bearers in the welcoming party and at the celebrations, and they all started out with oil. The tragedy was that when the bridegroom arrived five had ran out of oil because, through lack of forethought, they had no reserves. The wise virgins refused to share their oil in case they ran out during the feast. By the time the foolish virgins had rectified their mistake it was too late: the door had been shut and there was no place for them.

There is no doubt in my mind that the oil represents the power and supply of the Holy Spirit. This is the fuel which enables us to fulfil our task as individuals and churches to prepare the way and bear witness to the Lord's coming. If, for whatever reason, our contact with the Holy Spirit is lost, then we have no place or part in the marriage supper. These are serious words to all of us, whether we claim to be charismatic or not. We cannot afford to play around with God's provision; we must keep plugged into the supply. Our denominations and streams began in blessing. Historically, we can see the Holy Spirit at work in them all. However, when we fail to make his objectives our priority, we become apathetic or preoccupied with self-interest and the power runs out.

Renewal, restoration and revival

If we persist with God at this time there are, I believe,

three phases through which the Holy Spirit will take us – renewal, restoration and revival. These three phases are reflected in the messages of three Old Testament books which represent a prophetic trilogy revealing the process the Spirit will take the church through to enable us to reach our kingdom objectives. The books are Ezra, Nehemiah and Esther, and a few moments looking at the diagram below will help you to grasp the essential truth of each and the progression which leads us to our final triumph over Satan. Reading the books themselves will clarify the outline and a closer study will provide illuminating detail.

BOOK/ THEME	FOCUS	AREA OF ACTIVITY	MESSAGE
EZRA Renewal	THE TEMPLE Our starting-point GOD	HEAVEN invisible	INDIVIDUAL HOLINESS Each one must be in a right and active rela-ationship with God
NEHE-MIAH Restoration	THE CITY WALLS Rebuilding our base CHURCH	EARTH visible	CORPORATE RELATIONSHIPS Each one must find his place in the body of Christ and the whole church must work to-gether towards a common goal
ESTHER Revival	THE WICKED HAMAN The object of our destruction ENEMY	HELL disguised	EFFECTIVE STRATEGY Humility and obedience will ensure the ultimate victory

Ezra, in his account of the rebuilding of the Temple, with its typology, makes it plain that our first obligation is to ensure that we have a living personal relationship with our heavenly Father. In the current worldwide renewal, the Holy Spirit is putting repentance, worship and sacrifice back into the hearts of individuals who seeks God's face. As we make the repairing of the Lord's house and his altar our priority, putting worship back into its central place, we find ourselves at peace with God and his family.

However, 'renewal' is only the start, and in Nehemiah we see that we are to build not only with God but with all his people who share the vision of a 'New Jerusalem', wherever they are. The church takes on a new significance as the Spirit opens our eyes to the reality that we cannot make it alone. Uniting together to repair the city walls or, to put it another way, the 'restoration' of our understanding of church and its spiritual structures, will make us a people to be feared for there is multiplied power in unity.

Lastly, in Esther, our third book, we discover that Vashti, a picture of proud, self-sufficient institutionalism, will not be used by God to bring about the final triumph over evil. As always, God looks for a humble virgin bride to be available in her weakness 'for such a time as this'. With Vashti deposed and Esther in place as queen, we trace the development of a 'revival' which eventually completely frees the captives and destroys the enemy. The Holy Spirit, our heavenly Mordecai, oversees the coup; without him the task is hopeless.

Some have a difficulty in seeing 'revival' in the Book of Esther. I believe this is because they are looking at the story from an earthly point of view, in which case the elements we recognise in a spiritual awakening do not seem to be there. We need to see the story's spiritual meaning.

When we do this we find all the basic ingredients of the ultimate revival. Institutionalism is replaced with spirituality; the church, guided by the Spirit, gains access to the throne-room of heaven; the captives and those under sentence of death are released; the Enemy and all his cohorts are destroyed; the Kingdom is inherited in its fullness. The church must continue to co-operate with the Holy Spirit until this climax of history is reached, when Jesus and his church are ruling and reigning together over all things.

Therefore, as we yield to the Spirit, personal renewal and blessing will move on into a restoration which will help us to restructure our relationships and redefine our goals. Just as personal ambition can hinder renewal, so unyeilding tradition will hold up restoration. Any superfluous individual or historic baggage must go. Everything must be submitted to the Holy Spirit's scrutiny, as both renewal and restoration require hard work and changes in attitude and procedure. Together with the Holy Spirit we can do something about both of these first phases as they affect us and our churches. However, only God himself can send revival; it is his sovereign work, and when it comes the world itself and its institutions are shaken, and Jesus is given his rightful place in men's hearts and in their communities.

On occasions, revival comes when the church is unprepared. The effects of such a visitation are limited, particularly in the long term. The 'new wine' of the Spirit cannot be contained and the old wineskins burst. The Lord choses to work through his people, and if we are prepared with both Temple and city walls intact, then we shall reap the full effects of God's outpoured blessing in victory over our sin, the devil and death. Society itself will bear the marks and signs of God's presence; many signs remain in our nation today witness to bygone eras of heavenly favour. The realisation of these truths must surely drive home the fact that the only hope we have of encompassing the whole world with the gospel in word, deed and power, or at least reaching our full spiritual potential, is summed up in the words spoken to Zechariah, that great prophet of the Second Coming: '"Not by might nor by power, but by my Spirit," says the Lord Almighty' (Zech 4:6).

2

It's OK – it's in the Bible!

John

During the early sixties, a group of us who had been filled with the Holy Spirit went away as often as we could
during vacation time to the Elim Bible College 'to seek
the Lord'! The students were on holiday so there was
no danger of us doing them any harm. We were hungry
for teaching and one particular weekend we invited
Howard Carter, a Pentecostal pioneer, to come and
take the Bible study sessions. He spoke about
Zechariah's vision of the golden candlestick. We were
enthralled. We had never heard anything like it. And
after all these years I return, first, to this passage in
order to show that what is taking place around the
world is prophetically rooted in God's word. It lends
powerful support to my belief that, above everything
else, we must be filled, refilled and filled again with the
Holy Spirit if we are to see a church built which is cap-
able of glorifying God and completing the Great Commission given to us by Jesus himself.

Light to the world

Zechariah's name actually means 'the Lord remembers', and one of the great themes of his writing is the Second Coming of Christ. As in Peter's day (2 Pet 3:3–10), so today, there are those who feel that God has forgotten us, if indeed he exists at all. They look solely at the circumstances and suffering all around them, unaware that the Lord is 'not wanting anyone to perish'. They fail to understand that God works through his church and is waiting for his people to play their part in conveying his message of hope and glory to this lost and needy world. Were he to intervene now, multitudes would be excluded from the possibility of receiving salvation through hearing the good news of Jesus' death and resurrection.

Zechariah 4 opens with the sleeping prophet being awakened to see a golden candlestick burning brightly from oil supplied by two olive trees. The angel who awoke him asks Zechariah, 'What do you see?' Clearly, he is anxious to underline the importance of the vision. In the same way, God is sending his messenger to his slumbering servant today, but this messenger is no angel, it is the Holy Spirit himself, and his servant is not a lone prophet, but the church, raised up with the intention that we should become God's prophetic people. So what new thing is it that we see as the Spirit shakes us out of our apathy and indifference? It is not a literal candlestick. Quite simply, we receive a new vision of Jesus, the Light of the world! Everywhere, Christians who are genuinely awakened by the Holy Spirit are receiving a fresh revelation of our precious Saviour and what it cost him to redeem us. We are beginning to understand who he really is, what he achieved on the cross, and what he is really like.

The kind of candlestick Zechariah saw would have been made of beaten gold, hammered by the finest craftsmen. The incorruptible gold speaks of the divinity of Jesus; the oil, of the constant supply of the Spirit, which means Christ's life is an unfailing witness in the darkness of the world; the hammered work reminds us of his patient suffering. What a Saviour! Only saints who keep this vision alive will have the necessary incentive to press on to the end of the age, but there's more. Jesus stated in Matthew 5:14 that *we* 'are the light of the world'. Revelation 1:20 and 2:5 confirm this; the seven churches are described as candlesticks which will be removed if their light or witness fails. We are the light of Christ to the world; he has no other vessel or body here through which he chooses to reveal himself.

We are 'gold' or divine in the sense that through Jesus, God is alive and active in us; we are now his dwelling place. We too can be channelled in to that same endless supply of 'oil' guaranteed to us by the very same Spirit that raised Christ from the dead. That Spirit, even today, gives us life and empowers us, in just the same way as he did Jesus, to accomplish the 'even greater works' referred to in John 14:12. Not that we are better than Jesus, but the task is greater. Apart from the drastic increase in sin and unbelief, in our generation we have almost thirty-five times more people to reach than the early church. How much more, therefore, do we require the power which motivated them. I shall never understand why some Christians try to convince us that we don't need the Holy Spirit as those first Christians did. Personally, I go along with Joel and Peter who both assured us that in the last days God would pour out his Spirit on all people. They underlined the fact that those on the margins of the church and society will be touched and used when the Spirit falls. Women and children will be used by God – this was anathema to the Jews at that time as it is to some Christians today. Youth and the aged will also be included. No one will be allowed off the hook or to coast home. Every single saint will have a part to play whatever age, colour, status or sex.

Matthew 10:24–25 makes it plain that 'a servant is not *above* his master' but he can 'be *like* his master'. This brings me back to the candlestick and its hammered work. Every tiny dint in the surface gold – the finished object was covered with them – reflected the brightness and image of the flame! Each bruise acted like a mirror to the light. Jesus was perfected, or rather, he was brought to maturity, through the things he suffered. How can we expect our pathway to be different? Do we want to share his power and glory? Then we must also share the fellowship of his sufferings, and every dent or bruise which life inflicts, if we take it back to him, will be an opportunity for Jesus to be seen in us. We must not be afraid or shy away from suffering if we are to be his witnesses, reflecting his glory here on earth. Jesus suffered, we will suffer; Jesus triumphed, we will triumph; Jesus reigns, we will reign with him – all, and only, by the flow of the Holy Spirit through us.

A building fit for God

Zechariah 4 has still more to say to us. The background to the chapter is that the rebuilding of the Temple was being held up. The prophet Haggai, a contemporary of Zechariah, reveals that the people had become self-centred and lethargic. They were more concerned for the betterment of their own houses and lifestyle than they were for God's house. Their religion had become superficial and formal and the all-important work had stopped.

In Mark 11 we find Jesus in a similar situation. Jesus looked in on his Father's house, the very place where he should have been most welcome, and was so disgusted with what he saw that he left and went to Bethany. There he spent the night in a modest house with his friends,

Mary, Martha and Lazarus. What Jesus did not find in the Temple he found in the companionship he received in that simple home. Bethany literally means 'house of figs' and I hope you'll see the relevance of that before I finish. The next day Jesus journeyed back to Jerusalem and on the way he saw a small fig tree covered with leaves. Just as the previous evening his expectations had been dashed when he entered the Temple, so again they were now. He approached the tree expecting to find fruit, but there were no figs. The tree was barren and he cursed it.

For a long time I struggled with this story. The fig tree seemed hardly to blame as the Bible tells us that 'it was not the season for figs'. The action appeared to be totally out of character with the Jesus I knew who was neither unjust nor vindictive. It was not until I heard the explanation from a horticulturalist that I understood, and the significance of the incident dawned on me. This particular kind of fig tree produces fruit before its leaves are fully formed. The leaves are, in fact, an invitation to 'come and eat' in spite of their early showing. Because of the leaves one could justifiably expect to find fruit.

After rebuking the fig tree Jesus journeyed on to the Temple once again. It is impressive that he had not acted in haste the previous day, but allowed his initial anger to subside. In this way he had time to hear from his Father. Now he is able to act with righteous indignation rather than in an emotional outburst. Thus he ousts the money-changers and admonishes those who had made his Father's house a den of thieves. This purging of the Temple was a symbolic cursing of the old order which was all a sham, a show of leaves but no fruit, unlike the simple home in Bethany where Jesus was loved and fed. The Jewish leaders honoured God with their lips but their hearts were far from him. The structures were a total letdown to the poor and needy who came searching for

sustenance. Later, Jesus confirmed his prophetic action
when he prophesied that not one stone of those buildings
would be left standing on another (Mk 13:2).

The following morning, as the apostles passed that
way again, they saw that the fig tree had dried up and
were utterly amazed. Their amazement left them vulnerable, and Jesus immediately grasped the opportunity to
teach them about faith and the removal of mountains.
When I first read this teaching as a young Christian, I
completely tore it out of context. To my immature mind
the moving of mountains from one location to another
seemed a good way to confound sceptics. So my first
reaction was to give it a whirl – after all, you only require
a mustard seed-sized amount of faith to do it!

East London is not a particularly mountainous area so
I had to make do with a small hill for my experiment. I
closed my eyes and shouted 'Oh hill, be thou cast into
the sea!' Opening my eyes, I discovered that the hill was
still there; it hadn't moved one millimetre. I tried once
more, 'Oh hill, be thou cast into the sea!' I cried even
louder, but still it did not move. 'Why Lord?' I enquired,
somewhat disappointed, 'I'm only doing it for your
benefit.' Then the Lord said, 'Son, when I created the
world I made great mountains and small hills, and, for
the most part, give or take one or two exceptions, I put
them where I want them to be now. So, the last thing I
need is fanatics like you interfering with my handiwork
and moving them all around!' I was left needing some
other explanation for the story and it wasn't long before
the Lord graciously led me back to Zechariah 4.

Today, as then, and also in Jesus' day, a mountain
stands in the way of building a dwelling place suitable for
our great God. Pride, apathy, formalism, greed and even
lack of faith itself are all obstacles which stand in the way
of its completion. Of Western faith, Charles Price, one
of the first great American healing evangelists, said, 'An

army of emotions and desires has driven faith from the chambers of the heart into the cold, unfruitful corridors of the mind!' For so many, their religion has become barren, a Christianity of words without power, a *form* of godliness only. However, just as Jesus demonstrated to his disciples through the lesson of the fig tree that the mountains which hinder God's work can be removed, so the angel encouraged Zechariah, and so too the Holy Spirit strengthens us with the same belief. The mountains must, no, they *will* go, but how?

Our passage provides the answer, an answer which will be found repeatedly in the chapters of this book and which must also find a permanent lodging place in our hearts: '"Not by might nor by power, but by my Spirit," says the Lord Almighty.' The only way any temple will be completed, be it a literal Old Testament temple made of rock hewn from the hill quarries of Israel, or a New Covenant dwelling made from living stones redeemed from the pit of hell, is by total and unqualified dependence on the Spirit of God. Jesus reserved the right to build his church and he declared that it would be a church against which the gates of hell would not prevail. The work of building commenced when the Holy Spirit fell on a few disciples in the Upper Room on the Day of Pentecost. It has continued throughout church history with similar movements of the Spirit and will finish with the greatest and most widespread outpouring ever, and Haggai's promise, that 'the glory of this present house will be greater than the glory of the former house' (Hag 2:9) will be wonderfully fulfilled.

In the power of the Spirit

Today, the idea of a tired, weak and powerless church desperately hanging on 'till Jesus returns to rescue her is melting like snow in the warm spring sun. It is giving way to the glorious, biblical truth that Jesus is coming back for a beautiful bride, without spot or wrinkle, who is prepared and ready to meet her husband. She eagerly awaits him with her lamp ready and plenty of oil to see her through the dark night should he stay. 'Arise, shine,' cried Isaiah as he saw this through the eyes of faith over 700 years before the birth of Jesus, 'your light has come, and the glory of the Lord rises upon you' (Is 60:1). Peter, in his first sermon, leaves us in no doubt as to the extent of this blessing: 'You *will* receive the gift of the Holy Spirit. The promise is for you and your children and for *all* who are far off – for *all* whom the Lord our God will call' (Acts 2:39, italics added), and that means you and me, you'll be glad to know.

Just to be sure there is no uncertainty left in our thinking, let me remind you of Jesus' prayer in John 17. After praying for his disciples Jesus goes on in verse 20 to pray for *all* believers. 'I pray...also for *all* those who will ever come to believe...through their word and teaching. So that they *all* may be one...so that the world may believe and be convinced that you have sent me. I have given *them* the glory and honour which you have given me...' (AMPLIFIED BIBLE, italics added). How can we expect the world to see our oneness with Christ unless we manifest Christ's glory in both character *and* in power? Jesus passed the glory which rested on him on to his apostles, and then to the early church, and it is that same glory which he passes on to us today. No wonder there are still great expanses of the world in the grip of supernatural gods and demons, where evangelical soundness has failed to make any significant impact. The unevangelised are waiting to see the preaching of God's word confirmed with signs and wonders. Preaching and miracles performed in the power of the Holy Spirit are both absolutely essential to fulfil the Great Commission. Jesus himself did not manifest his glory only through grace and truth (Jn 1:14) but through miracles like the changing water into wine at the wedding in Cana (Jn 2:11).

Paul, in his first letter to the saints at Corinth, makes these statements about spiritual power gifts which are just as relevant to us: 'There are different kinds of gifts...but the same God works *all* of them in *all* men. Now to *each one* the manifestation of the Spirit is given for the common good' (12:4–5, italics added). 'Eagerly desire the greater gifts' (12:31) 'Follow the way of love and eagerly desire spiritual gifts, especially the gift of prophecy' (14:1). The work of the Holy Spirit is incomplete unless both the love of Christ and the power of Christ is seen in the church in this generation.

As I began to understand these truths years ago, I dedicated myself to Jesus and his church. It was my desire to work in partnership with the Holy Spirit, helping to remove the mountains which were hindering God's people from becoming 'the Temple made without hands'. In some small way I wanted to play my part by being available to God to serve the church, calling her back to her first love and her responsibility to worship Jesus and to be Jesus to an ailing world.

Soon I discovered that I was only one of a growing army of leaders with an identical concern from both within and outside of the traditional church. One of those men was Arthur Wallis, a father of the renewal who died suddenly in 1988. He was a good friend to me over many years and was tremendously respected as a Bible teacher. He came from a Brethren background and had a deep concern that our experience and teaching should be firmly rooted in the Scriptures, so much so that he made a study of every reference to the Holy Spirit in the New Testament before opening himself up to the baptism. The renewal has been accused of being shallow and with no theology, but those who made the criticism did not know the movement from the inside. Many fine teachers and scholars, like Arthur, went to great lengths to satisfy themselves that what they taught was thoroughly biblically based. Once they had established this for themselves they were willing to lose their reputations in order to stand for the new light they had discovered, whatever the cost.

The baptism in the Holy Spirit is widely accepted now in churches across Britain, and I fear that the renewal is in danger of becoming respectable. The pressure is on Western charismatics and Pentecostals to tone their message down. We are warned again and again of the dangers of 'experience-centred' 'Christianity as opposed to a 'word-centred' faith. We are frequently urged to get back to 'sound biblical teaching and exposition', but we must ask ourselves what sound teaching really is. Can any teaching which does not encourage or denies the full-orbed work of the Holy Spirit be described as sound? Please believe me when I say that I love the Bible. Without it we'd be nowhere, but if Bibles and sound preaching alone could bring revival, the West would have had revival years ago. In the UK almost every home and hotel room has at least one Bible and many Christians possess several. Sermons, tapes and books abound. No, the gospel of the kingdom must be lived, taught *and demonstrated*, as it is in areas of the world where people do not have access to teaching and resources. I come back once more to the lesson Zechariah learned all those centuries ago: '"Not by might nor by power, but by my Spirit," says the Lord Almighty.' There is no other way.

3

'Did you receive when you believed?'

John

When Paul first arrived in Ephesus he met a small group of believers. They were disciples only of John the Baptist but Paul did not know this when he asked the question which has caused so much debate over the years. He thought they were full believers and so his question still stands and has to be asked today: 'Did you receive the Holy Spirit when you believed?' (Acts 19:2). It is possible to believe in Jesus without having received the baptism or fullness of the Holy Spirit. This is just one area of confusion. There are others, about terminology for instance: 'What is the difference between being baptised, filled or anointed with the Holy Spirit?' 'Do I have to speak in tongues to be Spirit filled?' 'If I receive the Spirit by faith how do I know that I have received?'

I want to try to answer some of these questions, but it's not my purpose to be technical here. Paul's question was simple and straightforward. For some reason it was clear to him that these people had not received the Spirit in the way he expected. Amost certainly this was because there was no manifestation of spiritual gifts among them.

How else would he have known? For whenever the Holy Spirit fell there was some powerful, tangible sign of his presence and the fact that Jesus was alive and risen from the dead. So immediately Paul baptised them in water into Jesus, then he placed his hands upon them and the Spirit came. There was no time for a twelve-week confirmation or baptismal course here. How could he be sure that the Spirit had come? What was the sign? Quite simply, they all spoke in tongues.

Evidence of the Spirit

Now I hear your question again: 'Do I have to speak in tongues?' Why are some people so paranoid about tongues? Is it that this gift especially is an affront to trained Western minds? Frankly, I perceive it as a wrong question altogether. If tongues is indeed a gift from God, however small and apparently insignificant it may seem, we should be asking, 'Please may I speak with tongues!' If Paul himself found the gift so necessary and helpful (remember it was he who said in 1 Corinthians 14:18, 'I speak in tongues more than all of you'), why should we reject it?

But still we must ask, is the gift of tongues the evidence of the baptism of the Spirit? Personally, I consider that there is a strong biblical argument to support this belief, and for many Pentecostals it is essential to their doctrine of the baptism of the Holy Spirit. However, I prefer to see the gift of tongues as 'an' evidence, one of a number of possibilities which confirm that the Spirit has come. What I feel we must insist on is that there is some kind of evidence, by way of a spiritual gift that we have been baptised in the Spirit, otherwise we will always be wondering whether we have received the Spirit, or at least what difference the experience makes to our lives.

In 1 Corinthians 12:4 we read, 'There are different

kinds of gifts.' Paul then goes on to define the gifts and later in the chapter, in verse 11, he says, 'All these are the work of one and the same Spirit, and he gives them to each man, just as he determines.' Further on, in verses 29 and 30, he reminds us that not everyone has all the gifts. From these statements we can conclude that the Holy Spirit imparts spiritual gifts to everyone as he chooses; not everyone has all of the gifts, but everyone should have some, or at least one of the gifts. A spiritual gift, then, is the evidence that the Spirit has come in the way we are talking about.

If we are not clear on this, people look for other evidence anyway, and can be misled. I remember one of Europe's largest Christian Bible weeks where folk had heard good ministry concerning the baptism of the Holy Spirit and were called to stand for prayer. Hundreds responded, but no explanation was given as to how to receive or what to expect. A general prayer was made and those present were instructed to go out and do something they had never done before. I am sure those leading the meeting understood in their own minds what they meant, but obviously others did not. Some time after the meeting, a solicitor excitedly told one of our team members how he had been filled with the Spirit. 'I went out,' he exclaimed, 'returned to my room and at midnight I got out my shoes and cleaned them! I've never done anything like that in my life before.' True, what he did was totally out of character, but thrilling though it must have been to have shining shoes at midnight, I cannot believe that this is what the Lord intended to be the outcome of the baptism of the Holy Spirit!

Many Christians believe that they are filled with the Holy Spirit but the experience, or for most the non-experience, has made little if any difference to their lives. They may raise their hands in a praise meeting or jig about with the rest, but they could do that at a disco!

Many of these people are inwardly sadly disillusioned. Perhaps they are afraid to let the truth be known lest they let the side down by bursting the bubble. Maybe they were rightly taught that the gift is received by faith, but James, in his Epistle, makes it clear that faith without works – a visible indication of its presence – is dead. This is true for every experience of faith, be it salvation, healing or deliverance. If you claim to be saved but there is no outward change in your life, how do we know that anything has happened? If you are supposed to be healed or delivered but things continue as they were, what basis do we have for believing? Believism is as much of a curse as unbelief for both devalue faith; the one produces triumphalism and the other cynicism.

I say this not to hurt or upset, but in order to liberate and open folk up to the Lord once again to face reality and become spiritually active in their expectations. In this age, with so much emphasis on fairness and our rights, we constantly compare ourselves with others, which the Bible strongly advises against. If, as Christians, we don't have all that others have we tend to feel it reflects badly on ourselves or on the Lord. 'What have I done to deserve this apparently unjust treatment?' is a question we often hear. 'Is there some deep sin of which I am unaware?' 'Is God selective in who he blesses?' In the affluent West, the present generation has been schooled to expect immediate and personal rewards, but God often has different priorities and keeps the long-term outcome very much in view. We must realise that the Holy Spirit reserves the right to distribute his gifts as he sees fit, and he blesses and endows us all in his own way. Each one of us is unique and at a different stage of faith and maturity; he alone is able to take this into consideration. In all of this we are exhorted to 'earnestly and eagerly desire the gifts'. So why should we feel depressed or rejected when someone else is blessed or used by

God? This kind of response is a symptom of the self-centred society in which we have been reared. Rather, let us rejoice that the Spirit is active and at work in others in the church and let us see it as an encouragement to believe for more ourselves.

'Seek and you will find'

Some of us are just not desperate enough. We feel that God has an obligation to bless us. It is true that he has promised to bless and the Bible urges us not to put off receiving his free gifts. But it also declares that it is the hungry who are filled and that it is the seekers who find. There is a real tension here for God is not available like some genie of the lamp to answer our every whim.

My friend Phil Vogel, who many will know from his days as director of British Youth for Christ or at the Millmead Centre in Guildford, tells of his experience of being baptised with the Holy Spirit. He was not just uninterested in tongues; he was quite antagonistic to the thought of speaking in a strange language. He wanted to be filled but 'no speaking in tongues thank you very much!' So he prayed and waited, and waited and prayed but nothing happened. It was not until he was absolutely desperate that he cried out, 'OK Lord, I'll take it with tongues. I'll stand on my head if that's what you want. I'll do anything you ask, just please fill me with your Spirit!' And, of course, the Lord did.

If a 'take-it-or-leave-it' attitude prevails in some people, passivity is a problem for others. They have been beguiled into believing that because the Holy Spirit is sent by a Sovereign God there is nothing they can do about it. Yes, Jesus is the One who baptises us in the Holy Spirit. We cannot call him down or conjure up experiences at will, but we can co-operate with One who is neither reluctant nor mean. Just as we yield to the gentle pressure of the arms of the one who baptises us in water, so we yield and actively respond to and work with Jesus in order to be filled with the Holy Spirit. For example, it is recorded that on the Day of Pentecost they 'began to speak in other tongues as the Spirit enabled them' (Acts 2:4). The Spirit played his part and the disciples played theirs. Today, many reject the utterances they are being given as childish or jibberish and ask the Lord for other words which sound more authentic to them. Others are waiting for the Holy Spirit to come and take them over, to move their lips, waggle their tongues and activate their voice boxes, but he's far too much of a gentleman to do that. No, we must work together with Jesus as the baptiser, and with the Holy Spirit as the agent.

Years ago, when I first began to pray for people to be filled with the Spirit, I came across a Pentecostal man who had been waiting patiently for the Holy Spirit for four decades. Forty years previously he had watched the Spirit fall on his sister as she sat opposite him in her chair. Apparently she had done nothing except wait; now he was waiting. He was a fine man of God and had had hands laid on him. What could I say or do? I hurriedly shot up a prayer to the Lord and to my surprise he answered by giving me a picture. I saw a table laid with a plate on which was a fresh new loaf On either side of the plate was a knife and a fork. I heard the words, 'The meal is prepared, take the utensils and eat.' It didn't make a great deal of sense to me, but it was just what this hungry man needed. He understood perfectly.

That evening he went home and instead of waiting he worshipped and praised God on his own for all he was worth. Soon he found sounds forming in his mind and he fairly shouted out the words the Holy Spirit gave him. He went on and on speaking and thanking the Lord in English and in tongues for hours and hours. He was so overjoyed, he phoned me in the early hours of the morning, then praised and thanked the Lord some more. Later, he told me that he could hardly contain his joy at work the next morning. He just wanted to keep on shouting out all day with the new tongues he had received. And this was from a typically reserved and gracious English gentleman.

In early Pentecostal meetings people were taught to 'wait', or 'tarry' as they called it, for the Holy Spirit. This led to passivity in some. But they were also dedicated and enthusiastic people at prayer. They would sing and shout in English and in tongues in the ears of those who came forward for prayer. They would shake them and get them breathing in and out for long periods until folk hyperventilated and passed out. Others, in their ardour, would encourage folk to say 'da da' or 'ba ba' or even 'banana' backwards quickly and then declare loudly, 'he's got it, he's got it!' The strange thing is that sometimes they had got it. On and on they would pray into the night, sometimes for hours. We may smile, but one has to admire their dedication. I think if there had to be a choice, I'd go for the OTT approach rather than the passive 'God will give it when he's ready' kind of attitude. Tragically, people get hurt by all extremes, including the extreme of respectability and restraint which is simply more acceptable because the hurts caused by inactivity are less noticeable.

The 'tarrying teaching' was based on Jesus' command, 'Do not leave Jerusalem, but *wait* for the gift my Father promised' (Acts 1:4, italics added). This thinking is misplaced because once the Spirit had come, as recorded in Acts 2, there was no further occasion for anyone to wait for him. The Holy Spirit, having been given or sent by Jesus to his church, has been around ever since. This truth is beautifully illustrated through the story of Noah in Genesis 8. After the rains had ceased and the ark had

come to rest, Noah sent the dove out on three separate
occasions to see if the waters had abated. There is a deep
prophetic symbolism in what he did. Noah and the dove
represent the Father and the Holy Spirit. As Noah sent
the dove so the Father sent forth the Spirit into the earth.
First the Spirit rested on the prophets, priests and kings
of Israel but found no permanent abiding place and so
returned. Then he came upon Jesus, making peace
through the cross between God and man. Like the dove,
he returned bearing the olive twig. On the third occasion
the dove never went back to the ark. When Jesus sent
the Spirit he finally found a lasting home in the church,
his earthly dwelling place.

The water of life

What I say in other chapters will, I hope, help to deal
with any questions that remain. Here let me continue
with some more pictures. The Bible gives us plenty of
these as it is not a manual or handbook. Although the
character of the Holy Spirit remains constant, his actions
are often fluid and unpredictable. In Scripture he is por-
trayed as wind, oil, fire, water or a dove, not by bricks,
tables, jugs and static objects like that. Perhaps that's
why theologians seem to have such problems with the
doctrine of the Holy Spirit – he is indefinable.

If the prophet Isaiah's main theme is Jesus, and
Jeremiah reveals the Father's heart, then Ezekiel is the
prophet of the Spirit. Certainly he has a great deal to say
to us about the Spirit and the spiritual temple, and much
of this is in the form of visions and pictures.

One vision which is better known than others is found
in chapter 47. Ezekiel stood on the bank of a vast river
which flowed out from God's house. He was met by a
man with a measuring line who took him 1,000 cubits
(about 450 metres) to where the water was ankle-deep.

Again he led him on 1,000 cubits. Now the waters were to his knees. Once again he led Ezekiel on and the waters were to his waist. Finally, Ezekiel came to waters which he could not pass over. He had found waters to swim in, and wherever this river went, whether into the sea or desert, it brought life and healing.

Doesn't this remind you of the picture we find in the final chapter of the New Testament? John saw a similar vision of a river coming out from God's throne which was for the healing of the nations. What a contrast these strong, flowing rivers are to the buckets and foot pumps so necessary for irrigation in Egypt, the land of slavery. Human effort and striving have no place in the Promised Land into which Jesus is leading us. Perhaps these wonderful visions help us to understand better what Jesus spoke of when he cried out on the last day of the Feast of Tabernacles in Jerusalem: '"If a man is thirsty, let him come to me and drink. Whoever believes in me, as the Scripture has said, streams of living water will flow from within him." By this he meant the Spirit, whom those who believed in him were later to receive' (Jn 7:37–39).

As I said earlier, many of us are confused by technicalities and terms. Clever explanations don't really satisfy us and many of our concerns remain after we've heard them. Christine and I often hear questions like these 'If I have received Jesus surely I must also have received the Holy Spirit?' 'Why do some people have a powerful experience and quickly fall away, while others have no great feelings but go on from strength to strength?' 'If I have been filled with the Holy Spirit do I need to be filled again?' As we progress through this chapter and other sections of the book I hope these questions will be answered, but most of our questions melt away and are forgotten as we draw close to Jesus.

From the visions of Ezekiel and John, and the words of Jesus, we can begin to grasp the magnitude of the issue we are trying to understand. We are not talking about the physical world, intricate though it is; we are considering the Holy Spirit of God and the life of God himself. These are spiritual realities which we cannot fully comprehend in material or human terms; we need prophetic and visionary images to help us. Life in the Spirit is like encountering a river: you can paddle in it, wade in it or swim in it; you can drink it or you can drown in it; you can have it in you or you can live in it. This is awesome, frightening, thrilling and dangerous, all at the same time. It is a matter of degrees. You may have a sip and then go away, or you may drink deeply and go on drinking deeply for the rest of your days. You can dip in your toe and then run back to tell your friends about your experience, or you can wade in till you are carried away – then your friends will come looking for you! If you have a drink, the water is in you and goes with you, but if you walk into the fast flowing stream, the river carries you along in whatever direction it chooses.

The deeper we go into the Spirit, the deeper he comes into us and the greater the flow of his life through us.

Jesus said, 'If a man is thirsty, let him come to me and drink...' The tense here is the present continuous, that is, 'drink and go on drinking'. When we do this then, and only then, will the rivers of living water flow on out of us. There are many who have received life from Christ but they are not living and walking in the power of the Spirit. They have the water of life in them, but they are not living in the stream. Jesus, without doubt, lives in them, but they are not living and walking in the power of the Holy Spirit.

Sometimes it is very difficult to distinguish between the work of the Holy Spirit and the work of Jesus because there is such a unity between them and, of course, they are one in the sense that, together with the Father, they are God. Their aims and objectives are also similar in that they are working towards a common goal and harvest. We may separate them out for theological purposes but we will always encounter problems. Each member of the Godhead has his own individual identity and yet they are absolutely and completely one: not three Gods, only one, and yet three distinct personalities – it is a mystery! If we could fully explain God, he would have to be less than we are. Our finite minds will never grasp his omnipotence. So I revel in our limitations and rejoice in the fact that we can actually know him. The major difference between the work of Jesus and that of the Holy Spirit is that Jesus' work is clearly displayed for all to see, whereas the Spirit's work is hidden. Jesus, in the flesh, is the full image and expression of God, and the Spirit's task is to glorify Jesus, not to speak of himself.

Be filled continually

There are two aspects to the coming of the Holy Spirit into our lives, which are summed up very simply in two statements made by two of the New Testament's greatest characters, John the Baptist and the apostle Paul. John said, 'He [Jesus] will baptise you with the Holy Spirit' (Mt 3:11), and Paul instructed us to 'be being [present continuous] filled with the Spirit' (Eph 5:18). The first statement points us to a sovereign act carried out by Jesus, the second reveals what our response should be. Because Jesus *will* baptise with the Holy Spirit, we *must* continually be filled. I can do nothing except present myself and depend on his promise, but I have a part to play and I must exercise my will to receive and to go on being filled. He respects my free will and chooses never to force or coerce his followers to obey.

Many of us have received Christ and this is, of course, a work of the Spirit, but we have not abandoned ourselves to him. We reserve the right to run our lives and to take Jesus with us wherever we go. Others of us have hang-ups and are more concerned about what our friends or family think. Such fears limit and restrict us, hindering the free flow of the Spirit through us. Still others have confused their culture with Christianity, or even their denomination or tradition with Christianity. Thus whole areas of territory in our lives which are rightfully Christ's have been subtly roped off and occupied by the Enemy. So our release or filling or baptism in the Spirit, whatever we choose to call the experience, is limited. Are you uncertain as to whether or not you have received the Holy Spirit? Do you need a deeper release of the Spirit in your life? Has the experience you once knew dwindled due to neglect or restriction?

If the Lord has spoken to you in some way through these paragraphs, can I urge you to lay down your questions? Will you humbly acknowledge your need and invite Jesus to send or release the Holy Spirit to be your Guide and Comforter, to come and minister to you right now? It doesn't matter where you are. He is not limited by geography or circumstances, only by unbelief and wilful sin. Ask him to reveal more of Jesus and to create a deeper longing within you that you might be filled, or filled again, and so bring glory to the Lord you love so much.

4

Into the wilderness?

'Thank God for the baptism in the Holy Spirit, but to be honest that's when all my problems began,' is a comment I've heard more than once. There are at least two reasons for this. First, the Holy Spirit has not come to give us a quiet life, but to change us from one degree of glory to another. Second, Satan definitely does not like Spirit-filled Christians, so watch out. However, we can take comfort in the words of John in his first letter to the 'little children': 'Greater is he that is in you, than he that is in the world' (1 Jn 4:4, AV). It is true that we often misinterpret or misread the Holy Spirit's intentions for our lives. Let me tell you about my experience of being filled with the Spirit and what followed.

John's story

Back in 1959, Lilly and Len Allder, a couple who attended the local Baptist church, befriended Christine and me. The Lord was really hemming us in for, apart from these two at home, he had also broken through our defences at work in the form of a young Anglican curate from All Souls Church, Langham Place in London, whose name was Michael Harper. In the nicest possible way he and his wife Jeanne really socked the gospel to us. I was a rank backslider and Christine was a happy pagan, but we were seekers. Lilly worked in the supermarket at the top of our road and invited us to church and back for tea. To our amazement we discovered that they actually believed the Bible! Up to this point we hadn't met many Christians who did. On the whole we discovered that evangelicals were better than liberals; they accepted the miracles in history but chickened out when it came to seeing them in action today. But most of them were so miserable. Len just believed that the Bible is true and didn't try to wriggle out of things or explain them away. I was impressed and Len and I struck up a friendship. We both began to long for a blessing akin to that experienced by those first disciples on the Day of Pentecost.

Soon we heard that a pastor in the Bethnal Green area, who had been fiercely opposed to the Pentecostal blessing for fifteen years, had suddenly completely turned around. Now he was praying for Christians from all backgrounds to receive the Spirit and literally hundreds were! We could hardly wait to get along to his church and one or two other Baptists decided to join us. I felt like a shaken champagne bottle with the wire removed. When hands were laid on me I exploded without giving a thought to anyone else. I assumed that everyone was there for the same reason – to be baptised with the Holy Spirit and with fire! I'd not heard about observers. Later, I found them in the Bible, too.

It seemed to me as if thousands of volts of electricity were going through my body. I began to laugh and cry at the same time. I shouted praise to Jesus in tongues and then in English. I got up and walked round with my hands in the air. I knelt at the front and prayed for everyone I could think of and then started over again. Two hours later the meeting ended and we began to make our way home. It was only then that I discovered our other friends had left much earlier in total disgust at such a dreadful show of emotion. I was shattered. I could not believe that anyone could be in such a meeting without feeling as I did. Since then I've learned to respect and be more sensitive to the needs of others, but I wondered how our Baptist friends would have fared in the Upper Room.

I was so happy. It seemed to me that God had put his seal on me. It was as if he had given me an engagement ring and said, 'You're mine till we can get to the wedding.' I also reckoned God had found a bargain too. I sensed a calling on my life and knew my whole future was tied up with the Lord and his work. Now that I was baptised with the Holy Spirit, I could really get moving. I honestly thought to myself, 'Move over Billy Graham, you've done a good job, but now John Noble is filled with the Spirit. I'll start with Britain and move on from there.' Within a short time, I had created an organisation which I called Christian Enterprise. My motto was 'Christ For The World, The World For Christ'. John Noble was chairman, director, secretary, treasurer and office boy. It's a good job the Lord is patient with us and has a sense of humour.

In order to make an impact I decided that I'd commence my worldwide ministry by raising the dead. A few notable miracles would put me well and truly on the map. As there weren't large numbers of dead people lying around where I lived, I had to make do with second best – a very weak and nearly dead old lady. I explained to her relatives about James 5:14 and that I'd need some olive oil – the scriptural kind. They searched the house without success, whereupon I decided that God, being

generous, would allow a substitute. They returned with a
large bottle of cooking oil. I duly poured this on the old
lady, shouted some impressive commands to the sickness
and prayed one or two quite excellent prayers, leaving
the family with my full assurance that soon all would be
well. Three days later my old lady was dead.

Friends who know me are aware that I'm not easily put
off. At times, even in the face of obvious disaster, I have
the ability to soldier on against all odds. I did not intend
to be thwarted by the devil. I had a mission. It was not
until after I had prayed for two more old ladies, with
similar results, that I actually began to ask 'Why?'

The answer was forthcoming and in his time our ever-
loving and ever-gracious Lord began to help me understand. I don't remember the exact sequence of events,
but part of my discovery came as revelation through a
message which I heard Phil Vogel preach years ago and
the rest came through painful experience. I was taken
back to Jesus' baptism, the occasion when the Holy
Spirit came down on him in the form of a dove.

Jesus' story

As soon as Jesus had been baptised in water and filled
with the Holy Spirit, that same Spirit led, or rather drove
him into the wilderness. Unlike me, Jesus did not rush
around trying to drum up interest in his ministry; he
quietly allowed the Spirit to take him into the desert.
Jesus realised that before he could overcome the enemy
in the lives of others, he had to face him head on in his
own life. He would not be able to strengthen those who
were tempted unless he first overcame temptation himself. Now that the Holy Spirit had come he was ready to
face the devil and win! The contest recorded at the
beginning of Luke 4 is foundational to the whole of the
rest of Jesus' ministry. Let me explain. In 1 John 2:16 the

writer tells us, 'All that is in the world, the lust of the
flesh, and the lust of the eyes, and the pride of life, is not
of the Father, but is of the world' (AV). Here John identifies the three forms of allurement which our Enemy has
employed from the very earliest times. The devil has no
new devices. Within these three areas of seduction all
human weakness is embraced and all the temptations
known are telescoped. The lust of the flesh, the lust of
the eyes and the pride of life are clearly represented in
that first successful attempt Satan made on mankind in
Eden's paradise itself.

Genesis 3:6 recounts, 'When the woman saw that the
tree was good for food [the lust of the flesh], and that it
was pleasant to the eyes [the lust of the eyes], and a tree
to be desired to make one wise [the pride of life], she
took of the fruit thereof, and did eat, and gave also unto
her husband with her; and he did eat' (AV). Through this
forbidden tree, Satan attacked all of Adam and Eve's
areas of vulnerability and in one fell swoop brought the
couple down, together with the whole of creation for
which God had made them responsible. Sadly, the very
thing they grasped for through disobedience – to be as
God – the Lord would have granted them had they been
obedient. Had they done as they were commanded, they
would have ultimately discovered the tree of life in the
midst of the garden and lived for ever as friends of the
Most High. Now death, sin and destruction reigned and
held them helplessly in their grasp. They emerged from
the encounter in total bondage to their appetites, to the
material world in which they lived and to their own con-
ceit. To call this a tragedy is a gross understatement, but
let's return to Luke 4.

Jesus was not placed in a garden for his temptation,
but in a desert. He was fasting. He was not in the peak of
fitness; rather, he was at the point of starvation and mal-
nutrition, but he did have the Holy Spirit! After forty

days of denial, the Bible says that he was hungry. This seems to be an amazing understatement. A normal, healthy, thirty-year-old man can live without food for approximately six weeks. After five days of fasting one's appetite generally disappears. The body uses up all its natural reserves, then it begins to feed upon itself and its vital organs. At this point you're starving! Jesus, at his very weakest, faced Satan at his very strongest and overcame! He did not so much as blink in acquiescence, not because he was the King of Glory but because, as a man, he depended completely on the Spirit which his Father had given him, the same Holy Spirit who is given to be with us.

So, Satan came to this New Man with his old trickery, the lust of the flesh, the lust of the eyes and the pride of life. 'If you are the Son of God, tell this stone to become bread,' he said to torture Jesus' starving flesh; 'Look, all the kingdoms of this world are yours, if you bow down and worship me,' he claimed, fascinating Jesus' eyes, tempting him with a vision of what would only rightfully become his, as a man, through obedience; 'Throw yourself down from this high point of the Temple, you're invulnerable,' he suggested, appealing to Jesus' pride, offering him a short cut to acceptance as Messiah. But all his efforts were fruitless. Jesus stood firm. Where Adam failed, Jesus was victorious. Tempted in *every way*, yet without sin! No wonder we have a High Priest who is 'able to sympathise with our weaknesses'. Jesus has been through everything any human being could ever go through and more, and he came out the other side completely unscathed. Now, where we were doomed to fail with Adam, by the power of the Holy Spirit we can triumph with Christ.

The hymn-writer was wrong when he wrote of a *second* Adam coming to the fight. Paul, in 1 Corinthians 15:45, got it right: Jesus was the *last* Adam and the first of a whole new race of beings, quickened and made alive by the Spirit. In Christ Adam is put to death. In Christ we become new creatures, set free from bondage to a corrupt material world to live in victory in the new heaven and the new earth which God has planned for those who overcome. Can you see how important it was for Jesus to lay this foundation of success over the devil? By overcoming himself, he built a platform from which he could move out in ministry to overcome on behalf of others, this ministry finally leading him to his ultimate victory on the cross.

Jesus' wilderness experience ends with these words: 'When the devil had finished all this tempting, he left him until an opportune time.' The very next verse says, 'Jesus returned to Galilee in the power of the Spirit, and news about him spread through the whole countryside.' From this we learn that Spirit-filled Christians have to face the wilderness. Trials and temptations will come our way, but God will use them to teach us to become dependent on the Holy Spirit and this will be the power source of our lives. If only I had realised this earlier, I could have avoided much pain and embarrassment. However, this is a lesson I am continuing to learn and I praise God that he disciplines those whom he loves, so that they may more perfectly reflect his glory.

Christine's story

In order to keep the record straight and also to make an important point, I need to tell you about Christine's baptism in the Spirit. As you'll appreciate, we are quite different from each other and God dealt with us as individuals. Initially, Christine made the mistake that many other Christians make of looking at someone else instead of the Lord. She looked at me and all the noise, froth and bubble and said, 'You can't possibly have two like that in one family. The children wouldn't get a look in. I'll steer clear for the moment, maybe later, we'll see.' She had stereotyped the work of the Holy Spirit, was worried about the effects on the home if two of us were always rushing out to meetings and so clammed up. A few months later she realised that she was not making progress spiritually and needed a new dimension in her life. So unbeknown to me, she left our baby with a wonderful elderly couple who shared our house at the time and crept off to the meeting.

There she was, a fairly new Christian, with her heart pounding with panic as she approached the hall. I was helping to lead the gathering and she tells me that I looked 'mildly surprised' when I saw her come in. My surprise turned to elation when I saw Christine come forward as an indication that she wanted to receive the Holy Spirit. She went on into the 'receiving meeting', as it became known, and stood in line waiting for the laying on of hands. The pastor began to pray for people, but from Christine's point of view he started at the wrong end of the queue , the end furthest away from her. She couldn't wait and so with tears streaming down her cheeks she opened her mouth and in an atmosphere of incredible peace, she began to speak with tongues.

The experience was so different to the one I had had, but so appropriate for her. Far from pulling Christine away from the home, the blessing enabled her to give herself more fully to the home and the family. But more than that, as she gave our home to the Lord he began to send people to her for prayer. They were saved, healed and filled with the Spirit. I used to rush home from the meeting to find out what had been happening! Now, with the kids grown up, Christine is free to travel and the Lord has blessed her with a wide and growing ministry of her own.

In spite of my experiences, I still want recognition. I dearly long to be known for the deeds the Holy Spirit chooses to work through me. Like Paul, I want to be recognised in heaven, on earth and in hell for my relationship with the Lord. I now understand that this is on the basis of obedience and humility and that God exalts those who qualify, in his own way and time. I am also fully persuaded that power, in terms of spiritual gifts, important though it is, is not God's number one priority.

5

Happy and holy? Impossible!

John

Why is it that so many of God's people have the idea that happiness and holiness are incompatible? Yes, I do know that God, and not happiness is our goal. I also know that holiness precedes true happiness. But even so, is God a miserable God? Are we heading for an eternal praise meeting where the highest expression of joy will be when we lift our heels one inch off the floor as we lean forward ecstatically on the balls of our feet? Will we constantly hear the firm rappings of our Father's heavenly baton on his golden music stand, calling us to order if we look like singing Kendrick's latest more than the regulation twice through? Will our Father gaze at us over his pince-nez with furrowed brow as he constantly reminds us in gruff tones, 'If it wasn't for me, you lot wouldn't be here?' I can't believe it and my Bible does not confirm these kind of thoughts.

Joy that shows

According to Ephesians 2:7 we have been saved 'in order

that in the coming ages [God] might show the incomparable riches of his grace expressed in his kindness to us in Christ Jesus'. God's objective is to share his riches and to be kind to us. Over and over again we're called to 'rejoice', to 'be exceeding glad', to 'rejoice with joy unspeakable', and so on. And yet, at the first sign of any fun or emotion in our worship, we're told not to go over the top. (Actually, it is getting better. Have you noticed at lots of meetings now, you're allowed to enjoy yourself for ten minutes after the benediction has been pronounced?)

In the Old and New Testaments there are lots of words for rejoice. It appears that one word was not enough for the Lord! Here are the findings of one linguist. His name is Robert Young and his bestseller, *The Analytical Concordance to the Holy Bible*, was first published in 1897 and is still going strong today.

Rejoice (OT)	'to spring about', 'to gird on joy', 'to be joyful', 'to triumph', 'to exalt', 'to urge', 'to cry aloud', 'to bellow', 'to neigh', 'to lift up', 'to shout', 'to make shine', 'to sing', 'to cry', 'to shout for joy', 'to greatly rejoice', 'to sing aloud', 'to sing for joy', 'to cause to sing for joy', 'to make rejoice', 'to enjoy', 'to be glad', 'to make mirth', 'to deride', 'to have in derision', 'to laugh', 'to make sport', 'to mock', 'to scorn', 'to play', 'to laugh to scorn', 'to make merry', 'to shine', 'pleasure'.
Rejoice (NT)	'to leap much for joy', 'be exceeding glad', 'greatly rejoice', 'with exceeding joy', 'to make glad', 'to be merry', 'to make merry', 'to

boast', 'to glory', 'to boast one's self', 'to joy', 'all hail', 'hail', 'God speed', 'greeting', 'boast against', 'rejoice together with'.

In addition, I have it on good authority that the Greek word *agalliao* could be translated 'to throw yourself about like a lunatic'. So the disciples were covered for their raucous behaviour on the Day of Pentecost.

In Luke 10:20–21, after the seventy returned to Jesus, excited that evil spirits were subject to them, he said, '"Do not rejoice [Greek, *chairo* – 'to be glad'] that the spirits submit to you, but rejoice [same Greek word] that your names are written in heaven." At that time Jesus, full of joy [Greek, *agalliao*, a much stronger word – 'to leap much for joy or throw yourself about like a lunatic'] through the Holy Spirit, said, "I praise you, Father...."' In other words, Jesus said something along these lines. 'If you are going to be glad for yourselves, be glad about something worthwhile. Don't rejoice about your power over demons, but rejoice about your eternal security!' In the meantime, Jesus, filled with the Holy Spirit himself, yipped and leaped about just like one of Ishmael's 'glories' at Spring Harvest, because his followers were getting revelation! Who said Jesus never laughed or smiled, he only wept? He did both at the appropriate time and in the appropriate place. Many of us do neither because our emotions are locked up under a false mask of so-called holiness. Just as Jesus did, we are also commanded to 'rejoice with those who rejoice, and weep with those who weep' (Rom 12:15, AV). Sharing one another's joys and sorrows is all part of the evidence that we are living holy lives.

I don't know where we get our ideas about the nature of holiness from. Probably they are a hangover from the legalistic Victorian era. I call it 'negative holiness': the more things you don't do, the holier you must be. You don't spit, chew, dance, go to the theatre or cinema, watch any TV, drink, eat Mars bars, listen to non-classical music...the list grows with the years. Christine and I joined the 'negative holiness' club for a while soon after we became Christians. During the time that we were members of this club, I remember feeling that I'd like to take her out to celebrate our wedding anniversary. Nothing I could think of to do was safe or within the unspoken limitations subtly placed upon us by innuendo and insinuation. I finally ditched my last suggestion of going to a restaurant for a meal in case some worldly song was played over the music system. All that remained for us was to put on our best clothes and go to the Bible study as usual!

All this is quite out of character with the way Jesus behaved. He avoided religious people, choosing to mix with the common folks who enjoyed his company and humour and therefore received him gladly, so much so that he was wrongly accused of being a 'glutton' and a 'winebibber', although you can understand how the rumour started. His first miracle was performed at a wedding feast which, in his culture, could last for days. It was a miracle which most evangelicals would have tutted and muttered about for years. He turned 150 gallons of water into wine. Well, in fact he didn't, what he did do was even more unthinkable. He struck a deal with the waiters that however much water they drew from the six large jars during the feast, it would turn into the very best wine! None of your 'Boots' home brew or 'Plonks' end of the vintage-blended rubbish either.

Many saints who enjoy the occasional glass of wine feel guilty if they buy anything bar the cheapest, but Jesus produced the finest 'Galilean Cabernet', and the governor of the feast could not believe that such good wine had been kept till the last moment. How disappointed Jesus must be at some of our breaking of bread services. They are pale reflections of the meals he hosted for his followers where the fellowship was deep and intimate and obviously enjoyable. Here holiness enhanced the ordinary everyday interaction of those who shared a common faith and love for one another.

Apart from the fact that we hardly talk to anyone at our meals, many have actually replaced the bread and wine with substitutes, for example Ribena. Ribena, I understand, was actually invented by a Christian for just that purpose. In addition, in many churches we seem to compete to see how little bread and wine we can actually manage to take. The early church carried on the tradition established by Jesus, eating together and breaking bread frequently in their homes with glad and sincere hearts (Acts 2:46–47). These meals were obviously more than symbolic. They were a means of grace as well as times of joy and deep fellowship. To defile them brought serious consequences (1 Cor 11:29–30).

Going back to the subject of weddings, Christians generally don't like them unless we're in full control. Our holiness is brittle and might be broken in ungodly surroundings; we find them embarrassing and usually look for some excuse to leave before festivities begin. Our relatives are sometimes equally relieved to see us go. We don't view them as opportunities to show others how we can enjoy ourselves without overindulging. At weddings and parties Christine and I have had some excellent conversations as family and friends have been able to see the way the ordinary things of life blend together with our faith. Very often, when Christians are in control, weddings can be pretty barren affairs geared to make the unbelieving relations feel really uncomfortable. Our worship becomes stilted and unnatural, more of a show than a celebration.

Our eldest son's wedding was one of the most enjoyable I think we've ever been involved with. The legal part took place a few days before, at the registry office; we held the service and celebrations in a hall often used for Jewish weddings. Perhaps some of their freedom rubbed off – Jewish people have no problem blending their faith with life; they've been doing it for thousands of years. We used the ballroom for the ceremony, which was a great occasion. There was joyous worship and humour found its way even into the serious parts without detracting in any way. We prayed and prophesied over the happy couple. Everybody was involved without a wrong kind of pressure being put on non-Christian friends and relations.

When the ceremony drew to a natural conclusion we adjourned to the tables on the other side of the hall, which were already prepared for the wedding meal. There was no lengthy trek from church to reception which so often indicates that 'the religious bit is over, now let's get down to the serious business of enjoying ourselves'. Our love for fun and the Lord flowed through the meal and speeches. The family were clapped and cheered along with everyone else as the band played in the background. Finally, the meal over, we moved back on to the dance floor and sang and bopped the night away. A highlight of the evening was a tremendous sing-song in which old family favourites like 'Maybe it's because I'm a Londoner' were interspersed with some of our best praise songs. To anyone who had half an eye it was noticeable that Jesus had been with us all through the day, although we didn't need his intervention behind the scenes in the wine department – as far as I know. The bride's father, a confirmed atheist, said that it was the most moving wedding he had ever been to.

The law of the Spirit of life

Are you asking, 'What has all this to do with holiness?'
Much as far as I'm concerned because, in the name of
holiness, we have separated our lives into compartments,
which leads us into a kind of spiritual schizophrenia. We
are full of love for God on the one hand, and full of fear
to live for God on the other. When we divide the sacred
from the secular, we create real problems for ourselves
and especially for our kids and teenagers. We shut down
whole areas of life as being unspiritual and take away the
possibility of people seeing Jesus in us by the way we
handle living in those areas – in the world but not of it.
Setting up standards and laying down laws to keep from
making mistakes is easy in the short term and may even
be necessary for young children for a time, but trust and
maturity don't flourish under such conditions. That's
why Jesus did not leave us with the law. Good though the
law was, it could not save us, much less make us holy.

Jesus fulfilled the external law written on tablets of
stone, and introduced us to another law, the law of the
Spirit of life. The Holy Spirit has now come to live within
us and, if we allow him, he will enable us to keep this
new and higher law which is, today, being written on our
hearts. Holiness is an internal response and comes out of
a relationship, not as a result of an external command.
Yes, holiness *is* separation to the Lord as Bible scholars
tell us, but that separation is only possible when the same
Lord who shows us the truth about our sin and shame
also draws alongside us with his grace and forgiveness.
He empowers us within, enabling us to make the necessary change in our direction so that we can walk with
him. The happiness or joy of this beautiful relationship is
both egg and chicken; it is the root and the fruit; it is our
source and our goal.

Holiness that attracts

True holiness is, perhaps, one of the most neglected areas of the Holy Spirit's work in the church today. Much is taught about the signs of power and the gifts and there is nothing wrong with this, Yet very little is said about the joy-filled, holy life of obedience. It is my opinion that many of the problems and hurts that we seek to resolve by casting out evil spirits or through inner healing, valuable and necessary though those ministries are, would disappear overnight if we understood more perfectly what the Scriptures really teach about holiness. The path of true holiness may isolate us from the religious hypocrites but it will endear us to ordinary people who long for God and reality. The man in the street, for the most part, knows deep down that excess is sin, and many people crave deliverance from their compulsions. But such people also know that legalism and total abstinence cannot be equated with righteousness. So how can they be free?

The Scripture, of course, supplies the answer: the spirit-controlled life. Romans 7 and 8 are the great chapters which address this very question and they must be read in the context of the whole of the Epistle. However, the solution can be summed up in Paul's words in 8:14: 'Those who are led by the Spirit of God are sons of God.' Satan's first temptation of Jesus in the wilderness was prefaced with a question about his descent: '*if* you are the Son of God....' But Jesus had been 'led by the Spirit' into that very situation and was perfectly secure in his relationship with Father, so much so, that he paid no attention to the insinuation. Satan will also question our sonship, but if we are 'led by the Spirit' there will be a constant witness in our hearts to the fact that God is our Father. If, as God's children, we are to become mature sons we must yield to the discipline of the Holy Spirit who, in the words of one saint, 'will allow the devil to knock the hell out of us'. God is committed to seeing us grow up.

Thus the wilderness became a place of victory for Jesus as the Holy Spirit, having allowed Satan just enough rope, strengthened our Lord and brought him through the opposition into fullness and maturity. Likewise, those who trust the Holy Spirit to lead and guide will find that he will do the same for them. As the Master grew in wisdom and stature and overcame, so shall his servants come to fullness through a similar process. The principles don't change, only the circumstances. From this we learn that the baptism of the Holy Spirit is essential to the success of our ongoing, personal struggle to reach our full potential in Christ. We need the Holy Spirit not only for spiritual power but also in the pursuit of holiness. In addition to this we discover that holiness comes not through the application of negative law but through pliability and yieldedness to the will of God worked out in relationship to the Holy Spirit. We are never alone!

The Holy Spirit calls us, and empowers us, to emulate Jesus as he really was. He will not enable us to become like our particular stereotyped version, whether it be the ethereal, religious Jesus of medieval art or the white skinned, blue eyed, celluloid Jesus of some people's imagination. Producing holy saints is the work of the Holy Spirit; he makes us holy as he is holy. True holiness uncovers sin without alienating the sinner; it rubs shoulders with the real world without being tainted by its corruption; it purges wicked, religious systems and structures, but never stops worshipping the true God for whom they were built; it enjoys friendship and the company of young children and the aged, but it never allows sentimental relationships to block its ultimate goal. Because of the joyous outcome, holiness endures suffering and even death without becoming bitter. Holiness is

Jesus, Jesus living through us by the power of the Spirit, and holiness is totally and completely unattainable without the *Holy* Spirit's help.

My friend Kalevi Lehtinen puts it this way: 'Holiness is not a threat, it's a promise. It is not something you produce for God, it is something God produces for you. Why spend your life trying to achieve something which Jesus achieved for you 2,000 years ago?' All we can do is yield and co-operate, as with the Spirit's help we engage our wills and put off, with repentance, those things which he reveals need to be jettisoned.

Do you remember a lovely verse which we used to see emblazoned across the walls behind pulpits in our nonconformist churches? We were constantly exhorted to 'Worship the Lord in the beauty of holiness.' Perhaps we see it less frequently these days because neither our worship nor our holiness is very beautiful. Miserable, immobile saints who enjoy neither life nor the Lord are not the best advertisement or encouragement to worship. Another banner text we often used to see was 'The joy of the Lord is my strength.' In my naïvety, as a young Christian, I questioned the meaning of this because there was so little evidence of joy in the church. I was told by a frowning deacon that 'the joy is within, brother'. My conclusion was that it was so far 'within' that you might as well be without it.

The first of these great scriptures is part of David's psalm of thanks, composed after the ark, symbolising God's presence, had been rescued from the Philistines' grasp and restored to its rightful place in the Temple. David leaped, praised and danced in front of the procession. Michal, his wife, who thought his behaviour was unseemly for a king, despised him. The Lord did not see it the same way. In 2 Samuel 6:23 we read that Michal became barren as a result of her scepticism. Surely, as we see the context of this verse, it is not only an encouragement but also a warning. By all means worship the Lord as David did, with all your might, but cynicism will lead you to barrenness.

I know of one whole denomination which was birthed in revival yet rejected the new movement of the Holy Spirit. Once a thriving group of churches, thirty years later, it is almost non-existent. I believe that there is a very real link between our enjoyment of God, holy living and fruitfulness. The joy of the Lord and the beauty of holiness is attractive. Worldly sinners are not fools; their reasoning is that they might as well be happy and damned as miserable and saved. They see heaven as reflected in God's people and if it appears to be a place of gloom and severity, their simple reckoning is that it is better to be happy in this life and miserable in the next than miserable in this life *and* miserable in the next.

I am sure that some will level accusations of flippancy at me and cite cases where the charismatic experience has been abused and used as an excuse to indulge in festivity for festivity's sake. Now it would be foolish to deny this sort of thing has happened, but such judgements are usually subjective and mostly given from conditioned perspectives and reactions. This can be seen in the way that we will often tolerate in another culture what we would never put up with in our own. It's nothing to do with holiness but purely what we feel comfortable with, according to our background. I've frequently heard condescending remarks about 'simple' Third-World Christians as if to say, 'It's OK for them but not for us.' However, as the old adage has it, recognising genuine abuse when we see it should not lead to disuse but to proper use, otherwise every area of our Christian faith would be a no-go area, because every truth has been abused or misused in some way.

Through good times and bad

Furthermore, the joy-filled, holy life must never operate only when things are going well or it is not the joy-filled life; it is the partially joy-filled life. The joy of the Lord must function equally well under all circumstances. Sometimes it will be through the ecstasy of great blessings received, and at other times it will be through tears of sacrifice and pain, but always deep-seated joy will be the foundation of our strength.

I well recall the testimony of my friend Brian whose little girl was on life support machinery after she had 'died' during open heart surgery. She was brain dead. Her tiny mutilated body was there for all to view. There was no sign of life except the forced breathing maintained by the equipment. For six weeks he and Meg, his wife, watched their precious treasure lie motionless, surrounded by modern technology which could do nothing for her. There was no answer or explanation to the multitude of questions that haunted them day and night, but they cast them all upon the Lord. During this trial Brian went away for a weekend with the teenagers of the church. At the first meeting there was some embarrassment. How would they relate to a man going through such a tragedy? Their fears were quickly dispelled as Brian got to his feet, and with tears streaming down his cheeks danced before the Lord in praise of the God who he knew was good in spite of everything his circumstances told him.

Hezekiah had learned this principle too, as we see from 2 Chronicles 29: 27–30.

Hezekiah gave the order to sacrifice the burnt offering on the altar. As the offering began, singing to the Lord began also, accompanied by trumpets and the instruments of David king of Israel. The whole assembly bowed in worship, while the singers sang and the trumpeters played. All this continued until the sacrifice of burnt offering was completed.... So they sang praises with gladness and bowed their heads and worshipped.

As we offer our sacrifices to the Lord, however costly or painful that may be, we must accompany them with singing and worship. God is a good God and we know that in everything God works for good with those who love him. So happiness and holiness are compatible when the Holy Spirit is given freedom to lead us through the mountains and valleys of our life and experience. Go on, I dare you, delight in the Lord.

6

All good gifts...

John

The chorus of the old harvest hymn is true: 'All good gifts around us are sent from heaven above. So thank the Lord, O thank the Lord, for all his love.' God is a good God and he is a giving God. James confirms this fact in his Epistle in 1:17 'Every good and perfect gift is from above, coming down from the Father of the heavenly lights, who does not change like shifting shadows.' This means that God is not feeble minded, constantly regretting his decisions and doing U-turns. When speaking of the rebellious house of Israel, Paul, in Romans 11:29, declares, 'God's gifts and his call are irrevocable.' God does not go back on his words. He is faithful and his greatest act of giving is seen in the way that he freely gave us his most cherished possession, his Son, our Lord and Saviour Jesus Christ.

'For God so loved that he gave...' must surely be the most well known fact concerning God. Anyone who knows anything about our God has, almost always, heard that he gave his Son to die in our place and pay the penalty for our sin. But although this one act represented a pinnacle of giving which could never be surpassed, it is by no means the end of the matter. God is an habitual, unrelenting and bounteous Giver. In fact each member of the Godhead – Father, Son and Holy Spirit – is the same; they are all great Givers as we shall see. And we, God's children, are the primary beneficiaries. Let us first look at the gifts the Father gives. They are the natural gifts which were lovingly placed within us as we were formed in our mother's womb.

The gift of uniqueness

In Psalm 139 David clearly acknowledges God as his Maker in every detail: 'You created my inmost being; you knit me together in my mother's womb. I praise you because I am fearfully and wonderfully made.' David knew that he had not evolved from some amorphous blob which crept out of the primeval sludge. He was utterly convinced that he was not the product of some freak happening in nature but that he had been tenderly and carefully fashioned by his loving Father Creator. 'My frame was not hidden from you when I was made in the secret place. When I was woven together in the depths of the earth, your eyes saw my unformed body. All the days ordained for me were written in your book before one of them came to be.'

David drew great comfort and security from the intimate and detailed knowledge which his heavenly Father had of him. Every molecule and atom had been delicately woven together and planned. Every gift had been pondered over and selected with care to give pleasure to the one created and satisfaction to the Creator. David had not been cast in a die from which a hundred others just like him could be made. God is not in the business of mass production from some celestial mould, churning out thousands of identical items. No, David was unique, not even a short-run, limited edition. There was only one David and there's only one you and only one me, too. None of us will stumble round a corner one day and bump into an exact replica. This means that my sex, characteristics, temperament, gifts and abilities were all arranged by Father. They are not the outcome of natural selection. Of course, sin has interfered and marred what God made, but as I yield to him he's already beginning to straighten out those problems and, ultimately, even my body will be restored to his original design.

The peace and stability David enjoyed as a result of this knowledge and relationship to his Creator is in stark contrast to the frustrations and anguish which so many experience today as they suffer rejection and humiliation in our cruel society. Parents, who really wanted a girl this time round, or a teacher who mocked your lack of academic ability, friends who laugh at your shape or ridicule you because you're a Jew or black, can all be a cause of the pain. Is it any wonder that we grow up with all kinds of resentments and complexes? For the child of God all this is dealt with in Christ and is over; we are accepted and cherished. Thrusting aside worldly measures of beauty and excellence we can begin to revel in who we are in God. We do not compare ourselves with others, which the Bible warns us is 'unwise', but we rejoice in and utilise our gifts in service to the Lord and for the common good.

Early on in my Christian life I had to face the problem of comparing myself with others. I sensed a call to ministry and knew that at some time I would be serving God in preaching and teaching. At this point I heard a man called Roger Forster preach. He spoke for a couple of hours at such a rate that he crammed about six hours' worth of instruction into the time. He unfolded the prophecy of Isaiah giving us a panoramic view of the sixty-six books of the Bible from it's sixty-six chapters. I was knocked out. When he finished I caught a glimpse of the Bible he used. It was a wide margin version and every page was covered in minute writing with different colours for different themes. His knowledge seemed endless; he even knew about books like 'Expectations' and 'Hezekiah' which I'd never heard of! I was deeply impressed. I wanted a ministry like Roger's; he was my hero.

I purchased a wide margin Bible, a set of pens and some coloured inks. I bought myself a concordance and a nice perspex ruler and even a desk. Now I was ready. I sat down at my desk, laid out my pens, took the caps off the small tubes of ink, opened my Bible and waited for revelation. Nothing came. So I waited some more. Still nothing. 'Why Lord,' I cried, 'What's wrong? Have I forgotten something?' 'Yes,' came the reply from heaven, 'the brain son, you've forgotten the brain!' I was devastated and angry. All my school reports said, 'This boy has brains but doesn't use them,' so I had reckoned that they would be there when I needed them. But my teachers had lied and deceived me. I didn't have a brain at all. I was about to descend into a pit of despair and bitterness when I heard that inward voice again. 'It's OK son. I only want one Roger Forster and I happen to want one John Noble too. Just come as you are!'

What a relief! The Lord wanted me as I was because that's how he had made me. I had attended a highly academic school, gaining entrance by some fluke of circumstance and I survived by my own skills of leadership. I delegated my homework and obtained much better results that way, although exams tended to be embarrassing. Joking aside, my leadership abilities were never recognised or encouraged, rather they were seen as a threat. I may not have been greatly intelligent but I could gain the respect and following of my form mates, a gift which the Lord later was to harness and use for his purposes. Likewise all of your God-given talents need to be surrendered and available for the extension of his kingdom on earth.

Because so many of us misused our natural gifts before we became Christians, we tend to associate them with our worldly past. We are encouraged to put down the things that preoccupied us in our old life, which, at least for a while, we may need to do in order to lay them before Jesus. However, the Lord is not going to remake us as completely different people. What we gladly place at the foot of his cross, he will give back in resurrection life. He longs to anoint our gifts with his Spirit so that every area of our life is redeemed and can, therefore, be employed in worship and service.

I feel so strongly about this that I find myself full of indignation and anger at the Enemy who has robbed such numbers of us of our natural potential. Many wonderful saints are made to feel guilty about using their talents, as if their gifts are evil in themselves because they were once misused. Others don't utilise their abilities because they covet the skills of someone they admire. Some consider they have no gifts because they have never been valued or given any worth, and some are just plain lazy. Whatever the case, the Holy Spirit wants to anoint our abilities, however small they may seem to be. He desires to use them in a multiplicity of ways to glorify Jesus, bless the church and reach the world.

Cooking, car mechanics, administration, singing, embroidery, gardening, accountancy, hospitality, making money, and a thousand other things are all required by the Lord to impress his great love and diversity on our sick and twisted world. 'But they're only natural' I hear you saying. That may be true, but they are nonetheless *charismata* – gifts of grace from God. Ordinary people in the world may have such gifts, but where did they get them from? You may be able to develop and improve your gift, but you can do nothing to obtain what you do not possess. No amount of painting or drawing will make you an artist if you don't have the skill. God gave and, though he may not take away, he will surely call us to account if we do not use what he has imparted to us.

Let me give you one final illustration before moving on to consider what kind of gifts Jesus the Son is giving. My intention is to underline that even what we regard as being insignificant is useful to God.

I do not have a smile! On the other hand my wife has a smile and a half. Few smiles I know evoke the responses which mine and Christine's do. I am, basically, an extremely honest and trustworthy fellow, but find that people immediately become suspicious when I smile. Yet when Christine manufactures that smile of hers, which she is able to do at will, people would empty their wallets at her feet.

I have learned not to smile at customs officials. Whenever I did, they beckoned me over and spent hours going through my cases and belongings, only letting me go reluctantly, as if they were sure I must be hiding something. For a time I was quite resentful about this and felt that the Lord had been extremely unfair when he distributed smiles. Now I've come to terms with my limitations and realise that God gave me a smile in Christine and I've learned to work with her to use it to good effect. Believe it or not, when I had failed, for the umpteenth time, to obtain an entry visa to one particular country, after using all my powers of persuasion and those of my most notable associates, I finally turned to the Lord in desperation. 'Send Christine' he said, 'and tell her to smile.' After a two-hour wait, during which she grinned and knitted her way through ounces of wool, she came out of the embassy beaming and proudly waving my freshly stamped passport. Smiles, like all God's gifts, when used in the right place really can change history! So never underestimate the power or value of even the most insignificant gift.

Jesus' gifts to his church

The gifts of the ascended Christ, as we read in Ephesians 4:11, are clear. They are fivefold and are defined as apostles, prophets, evangelists, pastors and teachers. Much could be written about these gifts and it is my intention to cover them in more detail at some future date when I write about the nature of the church. So I'll just say one or two important things about them now.

First, these ministries, in particular those of the apostle and prophet, did not disappear with the early church as some would have us believe. The reason is obvious when we realise the purpose for which they were given. Their task is outlined in the same scripture and leaves us in no doubt as to the objective and end product of their work: 'to prepare God's people for works of service, so that the body of Christ may be built up until we all reach unity in the faith and in the knowledge of the Son of God and become mature, attaining to the whole measure of the fulness of Christ' (4:12–13). No modern business person giving a job description like that would be satisfied until the goals which he had set were reached. No more is God, and surely no one would suggest that we have attained that position. The church could hardly be said to have been prepared for service, reached unity of faith, come to the knowledge of the Son of God and become mature in the sense that, together, we measure up to the fullness of Christ in all of our life and work. As, therefore, nowhere in the Bible do we have the slightest indication that these ministries would be withdrawn, we must continue to watch and pray for them to re-emerge to complete their task. We must also encourage them and support them wherever we see them functioning in the Spirit of Jesus, the One who sent them.

Furthermore, let those who argue the case against apostles and prophets be consistent. For if these two ministries are no longer required, we must also dismiss the remaining three. On what basis can we retain evangelists, pastors and teachers when they are so obviously linked with apostles and prophets for the same purpose? Either the work remains to be finished and we need the special skills of these leaders, or it does not and they are redundant.

Second, the ministry is not an end in itself. The purpose of all leadership in the church is to train, release and encourage others to function. Those ministering are not intended to perform while everyone else looks on; they are called to do themselves out of a job. The church is God's secret weapon and only the church can accomplish the task of reaching the whole world in one generation. No exclusive band of super-apostles, or super-pastors for that matter, however gifted, could possibly do it; if they could, it would diminish the value of each individual member of the body of Christ. Perhaps those leaders who control their local churches, teams or denominations, demeaning the apostolic and prophetic ministries, should think more about making room for others and getting the leadership cork out of the bottleneck.

Third, these ministries are not open to anyone; they are Christ's gifts to the church. You cannot decide to be an apostle or a prophet. You may long to be one and that longing may well be an indication that Jesus is setting you apart, but there is no 'situations vacant' column. You can't apply for the post. Neither can men appoint apostles and prophets; we can only recognise, release and support them. There is no degree course you can take which will automatically leave you trained and

equipped; Christian seminaries have proved this time
and time again over the years. In fact, at one point in the
church's history, it could have been said that the church
was being killed by 'degrees'. Priests frequently entered
the ministry more as a result of circumstances or family
background than calling. And, contrary to what some
may think, I'm not knocking Bible colleges. They really
do have their place and, as with all aspects of Christian
life and service, that place is to discover what the Holy
Spirit is doing in the world and in the heart of the individual believer and then link the two together, giving all
the support and encouragement needed to facilitate the
God-appointed work. In the final analysis we are
partners together with the Holy Spirit.

Partners with Jesus

Partnership with the Holy Spirit is the key to a successful
life and ministry. Partnership is right at the heart of the
gospel, but the Holy Spirit must always be the senior
partner. Jesus spoke plainly about this in John chapters
14 and 16 where he revealed that the Spirit is our Coun-
sellor and constant companion (14:16), that he lives with
us and in us (14:17), will teach us all things (14:26), be
our Judge (16:8), will guide us into truth and show us
what is to come (16:13), and that he is our source for
receiving all that is in Christ (16:14). Through co-operation with the Holy Spirit we become partners and co-
labourers with Jesus himself.

The Greek word *koinonia*, which is usually translated
as 'fellowship', has the sense of 'partnership' or 'intimate
sharing' rooted in its meaning. The word appears, in a
slightly different form, in connection with our partnership with Jesus in three tremendously significant ways.
First, we are partners in his sufferings (1 Pet 4:13), second, we are partners in his glory (1 Pet 5:1); and third,

we are partners in his divine nature (2 Pet 1:4). It seems incredible but, by the Spirit, we can share in the very essence of who Jesus is, both at his very lowest as a suffering servant and at his absolute highest as God Almighty! What an amazing privilege. Has it actually dawned on us just how good God is? Why should we want to work in any other way but in partnership with him?

Partners with one another

Once we begin to practise this partnership with Jesus through the Holy Spirit, we can also begin to work effectively as partners together with one another. The Holy Spirit is the Spirit of unity and co-operation. Men and women can work in partnership from this foundation, as can black and white, Jew and Gentile, employers and employees, husbands and wives, parents and children, young and old, pastors and evangelists and of course, apostles and prophets. The Lord draws together those who traditionally polarise and oppose one another, blending their gifts for the common good. All can live in harmony and work side by side for the benefit of the church and its outreach. This is true kingdom living. With every wall of division broken down we become one nation under God to rule and reign with Christ on earth and in heaven for ever and ever. The great task of the five-fold ministry gifts of Jesus to his church is to release this great army of partners into the material world to usher in God's kingdom age and bring back the King.

In Romans 8:19 Paul showed us that nature itself is waiting with eager expectation for this appearing of the mature church. Every blade of grass, every flower and bird, every mountain and river is groaning and sighing, longing for the day when the 'sons of God' will walk the earth in power and victory. The trees of the field are straining, on tiptoe as it were, looking to see if this present move of the Spirit will be the final one that meets their expectations. And when the manifestation comes in all its glory, those trees will break out into spontaneous clapping and applause as they are set free from the curse of centuries. Poetry? Maybe, but if this picture is symbolic, the reality will be greater than the picture and I want to be there, don't you?

The way of love

We've seen that the Father creates and places natural gifts within us which we can use and develop to serve and glorify him. We have also seen that Jesus raises up servant ministries to help us function as a mature body. Now there is one other member of the Godhead who is involved in giving and he will not be left out. The Holy Spirit has vital gifts to impart and distribute. His gifts are equally necessary to the fulfilment of God's objectives here on earth. Historically, they have been much neglected and they are still a source of frustration and embarrassment to many Christians, particularly in the West. This may well be why we continue to wait to see the gospel effectively reaching and turning men and women to Christ in the resistant areas of the world.

As with the Father and Son, the Giver here also reserves the right to distribute his gifts as he chooses. They are indeed *charismata*, or free grace gifts, but after Paul has defined exactly what they are he says, 'All these are the work of one and the same Spirit, and he gives them to each man, just as he determines' (1 Cor 12:11). I cannot press-gang the Holy Spirit into giving me all the gifts or those I feel I would like, although I can earnestly seek for and desire them. There has been much argument over the years about fruit as opposed to gifts, and

Christians have tried to separate chapter 13 of 1 Corinthians from chapters 12 and 14. They call it the 'love' chapter. In fact, all three chapters are about the gifts of the Spirit and their operation. They must not be split up else we will lose their meaning.

It is not a case of love or gifts; love is the means by which the gifts must function and be used. 'Eagerly desire the greater gifts,' says Paul and then goes on, 'And now I will show you a more excellent way!' A more excellent way than what? A more excellent way than 'eagerly desiring the greater gifts'. Of course, there is nothing wrong with desiring the greater gifts but what is the more excellent way? Simply the way of love. If you say you love the church, you will want to bring prophetic messages from God to bless and correct. If you say you love the world, you will want to heal the sick and deliver the oppressed. If you do this without love it is of little consequence or value, at least to you personally. How many times do we read, 'And Jesus being moved with compassion...'? Every single time this phrase is used, we then read that our Lord does a miracle of some kind, or he sends his disciples to heal the sick or take authority over demons. Love will always lead to action. For this reason I sometimes doubt that what we call love is love at all, if it is not accompanied by some supernatural resolution to the problem which confronts us. The Holy Spirit distributes gifts so that we can put our love into practice. Love and gifts are inseparable; they are married – go together like a horse and carriage. You can't have one without the other!

Paul starts his discourse on the Holy Spirit's gifts with these words, 'Now about spiritual gifts....' There's the healthy ring of authority about that introduction. He goes on, 'Brothers, I do not want you to be ignorant.' That promises some down-to-earth, practical teaching and that's just what we get. So let's take a little more time to look over Paul's instructions on the Holy Spirit's gifts and examine what the Scripture says about them in the next few chapters.

7

Speaking of gifts – tongues, interpretation and prophecy

John

'Eagerly desire the greater gifts,' urges Paul, and his encouragement has led to confusion, particularly among humanistic and materialistic self-seeking Christians who, quite naturally, are keen to receive what they perceive to be the best, or greater gifts. Few pause to ask what they are; we feel that's pretty obvious. Raising the dead, healing the sick, faith (especially for large sums of money or houses) must be the best gifts. I suppose when your eyes are focused on personal needs and blessings these would appear to be the most important. We live in a society which is paranoid about death and health and finance so it's easy to assume that those gifts which may give us access to these things are the ones to seek after. But I wonder if this is true?

Perhaps, if we lived in a different age where personal success was not the priority, we might think differently. We might consider building ourselves up in our 'most holy faith' or 'giving glory to God' to be more important, in which case prophecy or tongues would be at the top of our list. Certainly, if the proportion of space given by Paul in 1 Corinthians chapters 12 to 14 is anything to go by, he considered the oral gifts of great significance, as I hope to demonstrate.

Of course, it could be argued that Paul majored on these gifts because they were the one's which were being abused, but looking at the rest of the letter I don't think that this was the case. The Corinthian church appeared to be generally over the top in every way, including in morality and church life. The oral gifts are important because they affect the heart of a church in that they endorse or undermine the teaching. After all, a sick person is either healed or not, but a false word of prophecy can bring deep deception and throw God's work right off course.

Concerning the highest gifts, my own feeling is that gifts are not graded on a scale of one to ten. Surely 'the best gift' is the one that gets a particular job done.

When I attempted to do my own handyman repairs, my favourite tool was the hammer. As a youngster I actually tried to put screws in with my hammer. It was much quicker and took less effort. I soon learned, to my cost, that the long-term results were not at all good and sometimes very difficult to rectify. I began to understand why Jesus was called *the* carpenter of Nazareth. It wasn't that he was the only one around but rather, because his work was recognised; he had a reputation. I pictured him patiently working at his bench, having learned the craft through submission to both his earthly and heavenly Father. He would carefully select each piece of wood and choose the correct tool to work it. The tables and chairs which he produced would have been top quality with no loose or squeaky joints. He always used the right implement for the job. There was no doubt in my mind that when he didn't possess the exact tool he required, he refused to improvise or bodge, but took his time to make or obtain what he needed.

This simple insight helped me to value the gifts differently. I realised that I needed to seek to follow the example of the Master who knew all the tools of his trade intimately as well as how and when to use them. With this understanding we will become much more team conscious as no one individual is a channel for all the gifts and a good team leader will be able to bring the right elements together to deal with each new situation.

Returning to the vocal or oral gifts. 1 Corinthians 12 lists them, along with others, in order to show us the variety of gifts and their source, the Holy Spirit. Paul then goes on to explain that every member of the body is vital to the healthy working of the whole. Each individual person who is baptised with the Holy Spirit is a precious part of the body of Christ. We must remember that this wisdom is offered in the context of teaching about the place and use of spiritual gifts. It is, therefore, concerned with the necessity of each individual to use the gifts for the health and welfare of the whole body. Tongues, interpretation and prophecy are given their place along with all the other gifts.

There are those who believe that, as with the languages given at Pentecost, all tongues should be recognisable and used to minister to foreigners in a way which they understand. This thought is obviously undermined by Paul's lengthy instructions in 1 Corinthians 14, but God does give recognisable languages at times. I remember being in a prayer meeting for business people in St Bride's Institute, just off Fleet Street in London, many years ago. My friend, Fred, spoke in tongues; another friend, Ray, interpreted. After the meeting a Greek gentleman approached one of the leaders. 'Where did that man learn to speak Greek?' 'Fred speak Greek?' said the leader. 'Sorry, no way.' 'Well, where did the other man learn the language so perfectly?' 'What, Ray? No, you've got it wrong.' The leader looked puzzled. 'He spoke Greek,' said the man. 'The other translated it and what's more they said things about me which no one else could know.' He left the meeting shaking his head, knowing that God had spoken.

Chapter 13 of 1 Corinthians underlines the need for love as the basis for operating the gifts, as we have already seen, and singles out tongues, prophecy and faith as examples. In chapter 14, almost 90 per cent of the text is on the use of the oral gifts in the church and 10 per cent on how to maintain orderly worship. Now, as I have said, it could be that the Corinthian church was preoccupied with these gifts. Certainly, they needed instruction in their use, but my belief is that these saints, who 'came behind in no gift', had grasped their value and were using them to great effect, although unwisely at times. Nowhere does Paul seek to curtail the use of tongues and prophecy. Quite the opposite – he actually tries to encourage these rabid charismatics into greater usage and closes the chapter with the straightforward injunction, 'Do not forbid speaking in tongues.'

I wonder what kind of instruction Paul would write to churches today, where our 'order' makes things so predictable that you almost need an act of parliament to rearrange the seating! Most ministers who regularly call their congregations to, 'rejoice together in the singing of hymn number 777,' would have a heart attack if their people really did start rejoicing! In spite of the many problems in Corinth, Paul claimed the church as his workmanship and said, 'You are the seal of my apostleship in the Lord.' Most of us would have disowned them. Obviously Paul preferred to clear the muck out of a stable rather than arrange the flowers in a graveyard!

Uses of the gift of tongues

Personal edification

At this point let me draw a distinction between the use of tongues for personal edification, and giving messages in tongues in a church meeting. These are two quite different uses for the same gift. In the first instance I am speaking or singing in other languages to glorify God and encourage my own spirit, alone or with others (Eph 5:19). On the Day of Pentecost, in Acts 2, the followers of Jesus spoke in tongues together, first in private in the Upper Room and then in public in the marketplace. This kind of use is advocated by Paul: 'Anyone who speaks in a tongue does not speak to men but to God.... He utters mysteries with his spirit' (1 Cor 14:2), and again, 'He who speaks in a tongue edifies himself' (1 Cor 14:4). So here is another reason why we should encourage everyone to believe that God desires us all to use the gift in this way. Do only some of us need to edify ourselves? Are the rest so close to God that the gift is of no relevance? Personally, I go along with Paul when he says 'I thank God that I speak in tongues more than all of you' (1 Cor 14:18). Some linguists say that this means 'more than you all put together'. I guess that on those long, lonely journeys, Paul would spend much of his time speaking to God and building himself up by exercising this powerful and blessed gift.

He also plainly urges them, 'I would like every one of you to speak in tongues' (1 Cor 14:5). I need to point out here that we are not talking about one language each! Included in the list of gifts in 1 Corinthians 12 are the words: 'To another [singular]...different kinds of tongues [plural]', (12:10), and later we find them described as 'the tongues of men and angels' (13:1). Many who speak in tongues restrict themselves to their safe areas and have no expectation of increasing their vocal abilities. It's amazing how quickly the Enemy puts fences up around us. We're free to speak in tongues providing it sounds like something we've heard someone else speak, or maybe if we think it sounds like Greek or Hebrew. So we limit ourselves to, say, the 'karrakashee, karracasha,' type of sounds.

I'll never forget one occasion when I was driving alone in the car. I was going through quite a difficult time and my prayers were bouncing off the heavens as though they were made of brass. So I started to pray and shout in tongues. Slowly but surely I broke through and joy flooded the car. I got so excited I began to speak in a completely strange language. It sounded to me as if it had come from the depths of the African jungle. 'Ooala wambu nyongula barada', or something like that. The dark atmosphere left and the car was filled with the presence of God. Then the Lord simply asked me, 'Would you use that tongue when you praise me in a church meeting?' Immediately I felt embarrassed, but got the message. If the devil can't stop us from speaking in tongues, he'll restrict us to using one language or even just a few words. Break out of the mould he has forced you into and bless God in every way you can.

Apart from restricting us, the Enemy also wants to discredit the gifts or plant fear in our minds. Every now and again we hear stories about people swearing or speaking evil things in tongues. Of course this will happen if someone is motivated by evil spirits, but not if our hearts are directed towards Jesus. Sometimes a limited understanding of a language can be a disadvantage, as the same word can mean something totally different in another tongue. This can be startlingly demonstrated in the problems we have between English and American English, for example words like pants, boot, bum, etc. Someone has said that the English and Americans are divided by a common language!

Peter Dippl, a pastor in Berlin, had a disturbing experience in a gathering of three hundred leaders. A message came in tongues and before the interpretation could be given some one shouted out, 'That language was Sanscrit, I recognise it! A word referred to the devil and it is not of God.' A hush came on the meeting and you could sense the apprehension. Peter wisely turned to the man and asked him what else the message contained, but his knowledge of the language was very poor, so Peter asked for the interpretation to be given. Someone gave it: 'The work of Satan and demon spirits abound, but Jesus is victorious over all these powers....' A tangible relief spread round the room, a little knowledge can be a dangerous thing!

In Ephesians 5:18–21 Paul precedes the words 'Submit to one another out of reverence to Christ' with, 'Do not get drunk on wine.... Be filled with the Spirit.' The inference here is that the effects of the Holy Spirit and wine are similar in terms of making one feel happy and joyful, but the Holy Spirit leads us to respect one another, and to blessing rather than abuse and debauchery. He goes on, 'Speak to one another with psalms, hymns and spiritual songs', making it plain that it is important to edify ourselves in spirit if we are to succeed in submitting to one another. He then takes the whole matter further instructing 'husbands, love your wives as Christ loved the church', 'wives, submit to your husbands as to the Lord', 'children, obey your parents', 'slaves [in our society read employees], obey your earthly masters with respect' and 'masters [read employers], treat your slaves in the same way.' This capacity to love, serve and honour is the result of the Holy Spirit's presence in our lives. Consistently choosing to act in this way is the fuel which keeps us running smoothly. The Spirit enables us to exercise our wills, in order to decide to live in harmony and truth. There is a flowing circle of receiving and action, both of

which are necessary if we are to retain the fullness of the
Spirit, and both of which are dependent on him.

How can the newly married Juliet submit to her
Romeo when she discovers he doesn't wash properly or
change his underwear? When his feet are like blocks of
ice and he never cuts his toenails which scrape the backs
of her legs as he creeps into bed late from watching the
world cup 'till the early hours? Well, one way is through
reaching deep within herself to those hidden wells of
spirituality by speaking and edifying herself quietly
under her breath in tongues! How can Romeo love his
Juliet as Christ loved the church when she puts on that
egg-stained dressing gown and slops about in slippers
two sizes too big as she burns the toast for the third
morning in a row? Again, by lifting his eyes and voice to
heaven and building himself up as he cries out in another
language. Kids with unreasonable parents, who ask them
to do what they would never attempt; employees on
Monday morning stuck in a traffic jam; business men facing unrelenting bank managers – all need this glorious
contact with the Holy Spirit which comes through singing
and praying in tongues.

I guess some people will accuse me of trivialising the
gift of tongues. But often it's the 'little foxes that gnaw
the vines'. We tend not to trip over boulders; it's the
bumps in the path that cause us trouble. The Holy Spirit
is there to help us through all life's trials be they large or
small.

So this first application of the use of tongues is for personal upbuilding. I may do this by praying or by singing
with my spirit (1 Cor 14:15); my mind does not benefit
but my spirit does (1 Cor 14:14). I may do this alone or
together with others, as the disciples did on that first Day
of Pentecost and as the Corinthian church did.

A sign for unbelievers

Even though unbelievers may feel that we are 'out of our minds' (1 Cor 14:23), tongues is, nevertheless, a sign for them. After quoting Isaiah 28:11–12 – 'with foreign lips and strange tongues God will speak to his people,' – Paul categorically states, 'Tongues, then, are a sign, not for believers but for unbelievers.' They may think we're nuts but they are fascinated, often moved and sometimes converted when they hear these weird and wonderful sounds, especially when there are thousands of us blending our voices together, apparently without a conductor. And there's nothing new about unbelievers thinking we're mad. Paul has already argued along those lines in connection with the cross and the gospel itself in this self-same letter.

I do believe that verses 20-25 of 1 Corinthians 14 present some difficulties, as Paul appears to contradict himself. No doubt if we were to examine all the theories concerning his meaning we'd need another chapter at the very least. My own view is that Paul is drawing a distinction between antagonistic, well versed, sceptics and totally unreached people who were likely to be open and sympathetic to the supernatural. Either way his statement is confirmed by what happened on the Day of Pentecost.

Furthermore, the value of joining together to worship God with our tongues is demonstrated in Acts 2. As the 120 believers praised God in the marketplace a crowd came together. When Peter stood up and preached, 3,000 were saved. 'Ah,' I hear you saying, 'they spoke in recognisable tongues, that's acceptable, but it's not right to speak out publicly in tongues which cannot be understood!' It is true that at least some of the languages were comprehensible, but how could those disciples have known before they spoke what language they would use? As they praised God together, the Holy Spirit inspired the utterances; he was in control. That is why I maintain that corporate worship in tongues can be used by God in evangelism. Some have said that love would keep us from using tongues in public in this way. Certainly, love would not arrogantly parade the gifts or use them to draw attention to oneself, but neither would love deny people the opportunity of being onlookers as the people of God give him the beautiful praise and worship which is his due.

To bring messages to the church

To what, then, is Paul referring when he makes statements such as, 'In the church I would rather speak five intelligible words to instruct others than ten thousand words in a tongue' (1 Cor 14:19), or, 'If there is no interpreter, the speaker [in tongues] should keep quiet in the church and speak to himself and God' (1 Cor 14:28), and 'Do all speak in tongues?' (1 Cor 12:30). Once again, one must look at the context in which these instructions were given and put them alongside other teaching given here and examples or experiences elsewhere in Scripture. At the end of chapter 12 Paul is talking about the gifts functioning within the body, and in chapter 14 he is developing the theme of order in church services.

Although everyone may speak in tongues to glorify God and edify themselves, not everyone has the gift of bringing messages in tongues to the whole church. Even if everyone had such a gift, what use is it unless there is an interpreter? This argument comes through in various places throughout the chapter. It is very clear that these enthusiastic, often imprudent saints at Corinth were so excited with their tongues speaking that they were putting on a 'tongues spectacular'. One by one they would display their new-found abilities, perhaps going from one kind of language to another. It may have been great fun for a while but soon it became boring, and anyway it was totally unproductive and therefore time-wasting.

So Paul laid down a few simple guidelines in 1 Corinthians 14. First, 'I'd rather you prophesied than spoke in tongues unless you, or someone else interprets' (14:4–5, 27). Second, 'Tongues and interpretation are not necessarily the same as prophecy as the one who speaks in tongues speaks to God' (14:2). Third, 'When you speak in tongues let two or three at a time speak and then there must be an interpreter' (14:27). Fourth, 'If at any time anyone does speak in tongues and there is no one to interpret pray for the interpretation' (14:13). Fifth, 'The purpose of all this is to upbuild and strengthen the church' (14:4, 12, 26). Sixth, 'Tongues without interpretation is certainly less than prophecy' (14:5). We see, then, that there is a special use of tongues for the individual – to bring spiritual messages – provided there is an interpreter. Not everyone has this gift; it is for the strengthening, edifying and upbuilding of the whole church, and the gift should function in an orderly and understandable fashion.

The interpretation of tongues

It may be necessary here to underline the fact that an interpretation is not a translation. The one who interprets does not automatically translate word-for-word, what has been said, but feels and expresses the heart of the message. This explains why the interpretation is sometimes shorter or longer than the message itself. As I have suggested, such messages will not always be God speaking to the church; perhaps more often they will be the overflow of the joys or concerns of the messenger who 'does not speak to men but God' (14:2). For example, 'My heart rejoices in the goodness of the Lord...', or, 'I am filled with sorrows and my soul cries out as I feel God's pain for....' Personally, I can see no reason why more than one individual should not be involved in bringing or amplifying an interpretation. Furthermore, it is often difficult to determine where interpretation stops and prophecy begins; they may well flow into one another as the one who interprets picks up the burden and takes it on. Maybe this leads us on to talk a little about prophecy and prophets.

Prophets and prophecy

To begin with, let me tell you a story to illustrate the power of a simple prophetic word. Danny Smith, a journalist, found himself giving more and more of his time to the needs of the suffering church. God had used him in the 'Free the Siberian Seven' campaign, and the burden he carried would just not go away. Many questions faced him as he thought about his future and the possibility of giving up his regular job, which would leave him with very little support of any kind. One group who had blessed Danny and his work was the Cobham Christian Fellowship.

Danny and his wife Joan visited the group to say 'thank you', with Timothy Chmykalov, one of the 'Seven'. At the close of the meeting Gerald Coates, founder of the fellowship, prayed and prophesied over Danny and Joan. 'You have many friends all over the world but now God is asking you to find your real friends. This is a time for you to build friendships to nurture you for the next stage of your ministry.' They burst into tears and wept publicly. Gerald had no idea that all the way to the meeting they had been asking 'Who are our real friends', and 'Who can we trust?' The outcome was that they moved to Cobham and with Gerald's help set up the Jubilee Campaign which today has 150 MPs campaigning for prisoners of faith throughout the world.

There is not space here to do justice to the ministry of the prophet. But I do need to clear up one common mis-understanding. Prophesying and being a prophet are not always the same thing. In fact, a prophet does not even have to speak to be a prophet! In a prophet two things come together: his life and his message. A prophet does not just deliver a message; he lives it and sometimes suffers deeply in the process. Prophets and martyrdom often go together. The first prophet in the Bible was Abel, who did not speak at all yet he was murdered as a result of his prophetic action. Hebrews 11:4 declares that 'By faith he still speaks, even though he is dead.' Prophets constantly bring people face to face with God's truth and grace by their lives, words and deeds. The prophet is the ministry. In the same way that we may all sing or move our bodies, but that does not necessarily make us singers or dancers, so we may all prophesy (1 Cor 14:31), but that does not automatically mean that we are all prophets (1 Cor 12:29). And the spirit of a prophet is subject to control (1 Cor 14:32). No one is so anointed, no word so important, that the prophet is taken over and forced to speak or unable to stop himself.

As I write these pages I am aware that in the next year or two we shall see a tremendous amount of time and attention being given to prophets and prophecy. I reckon there will be much blessing, but some terrible mistakes made, which will force us into a greater understanding of the ministry. I believe that this will also press us to look closer at the character and role of the apostle, which we will finally see as being a key to the full release of all the other ministries.

For the moment, let me say that many of those who are used in what some call 'personal prophecy', or giving words to individuals and churches about their future, may, in fact, prove to be gifted in prophesying or words of knowledge and wisdom, rather than actually being prophets. Because of the sensational nature of the gift, they receive the acclaim and recognition of being prophets, which can give us a wrong expectation and a failure to understand their limitations. Jamie Buckingham has pointed out that some of us men are more ready to hear God speaking through a prophet than we are to hear him speaking through our wives. However, we must not write off prophets when we come across abuse or the Enemy will have scored a direct hit on the proper structure of church leadership.

It may help us at this juncture to search out and study the qualities of a prophet so that we can begin to recognise them and give them the place and respect they deserve.

Just let me interject here three words which hopefully will help us move in the right direction in this respect – foundations, holiness and justice. Prophets in both the Old and New Testaments were heavily involved in all of these matters. This means that the mental picture of a prophet being unstable, extra-sensitive and insecure is wrong. Prophets may be emotional and feel much pain, but to keep God's people on track requires strength, stability and determination.

Testing prophecy

When a major prophetic word is given which could change or shape the future direction of a church or movement, it is important to properly weigh and test its validity. There is no betrayal or lack of faith expressed in taking these steps. Too many heavy or demanding words have been given without the proper endorsement. Some of these have been discredited; many have conveniently been forgotten. Either way damage results as God's work and people are hurt. It is good to transcribe such a word so that there can be no doubt what has been said and then at least three groupings should be consulted and called to prayer: the church itself, the local leadership with pastors and teachers, and the extra-local ministries in relationship, that is, the apostles and prophets or others who have some oversight responsibilities. In a traditional church setting these latter may be a respected superintendent or bishop. This shows that we treat prophecy seriously but are unwilling to move without clear confirmation and a measure of unity.

When we are used by the Lord to bring a powerful prophetic message, it is very easy to become proud and get a false sense of our importance. We may begin to act and speak with an authority way beyond us and despise anyone who challenges us or questions our words. This is evidently wrong, for although Scripture tells us 'Do not treat prophecies with contempt' (1 Thess 5:20), the next verse urges us to test or judge them.

Paul's instruction shows us that the high expectation of 100 per cent accuracy, which some have of those who prophesy, is unreasonable. If the gift is always completely accurate why should we be required to judge it? 1 Corinthians 13:9 confirms that 'we prophesy in part', or 'incompletely and imperfectly' according to the Amplified Bible. If this were not so prophecy would be on a par with Scripture, which it is not. It is, therefore, very important that we weigh prophecy. The fact that certain people declare their words to be from God does not mean that the rest of us are forbidden the right to examine them or look for confirmation elsewhere. On the contrary, I would go so far as to say that we should always expect prophetic direction to be confirmed in some way, but I shall return to the matter of handling prophecy later.

The prophet's ministry

Some people who prophesy fancy themselves as Old Testament-style prophets; the idea appeals to their ego and sometimes they have a martyr complex to go with it. They may even dress in a strange way in an attempt to prove a point. However, in the New Testament the prophet's ministry is not quite the same as it was in the Old Testament. Through the death and resurrection of Jesus a subtle change has come. After the Gospels you do not find those rugged individualists, as the prophet's ministry is from within, and to, the church. Prophets, along with apostles, are foundational to the building up of the church (Eph 2:20). Since Jesus was 'the great Prophet', and was also the fulfilment of the Old Testament law and prophets, and we, the church, are now his body on earth, God has appointed us corporately to be 'the prophet' today, or better, 'a prophetic people'. Together, by our words, works and wonders, we are to be a manifestation of 'Christ the Prophet' in the world, and our highest calling is to share the fellowship of his sufferings, his death and his glory. New Testament prophets are, of course, important to God's plan, but they are to devote themselves to, and pour their ministry into, the church. Their task is to bring her to fullness and maturity, together with apostles, evangelists, pastors and teachers. They are not called to be eccentric superstars drawing attention to themselves.

Paul highlights the importance of prophets and prophecy throughout 1 Corinthians 14. Those who prophesy strengthen, encourage and comfort (14:3); they edify the church (14:4); they are greater than those who only speak with tongues (14:5) and they bring conviction to unbelievers (14:24–25). Paul goes on to encourage orderly sessions of prophetic ministry, with two or three prophets speaking and then others weighing what has been said (14:29). He makes it clear that no one who prophesies is so driven by the Holy Spirit that he cannot give place to another. The Holy Spirit should be allowed to orchestrate the revelations (14:30, 32), 'You can all prophesy in turn so that everyone may be instructed and encouraged' (14:31). Finally, he finishes his instruction with these words; 'Brothers, be eager to prophesy' (14:39).

However, in Romans 12:6 Paul gives us one more important piece of advice: 'If a man's gift is prophesying, let him use it in proportion to his faith.' You may feel the counsel to be obvious, but it is easy to ignore. A friend of mine was feeling rather low during a meeting and some- one made a simple prophecy over him. 'The Lord knows what you are going through, he is with you and will bring you into a new place of blessing.' That is the gist of it and it was just the right word. The one who brought the prophecy was so encouraged by the change he saw that he decided to go on. 'Indeed, the Lord will greatly bless you and you will see many miracles. The sick will be healed and, verily, the dead raised. Yea, many dead will be raised.' he cried, reaching a crescendo! But he had moved from the Spirit into the flesh, and even the bles- sing was lost as my friend could no longer believe any of what had been said. Surely, we are well advised to work within the measure of faith we have been granted.

The Corinthian church may have been over the top, but it's much easier to give direction to a moving object than a stationary one. Putting some order into the Corinthian chaos was a lot simpler than trying to inject life into our orthodox order. Leaving aside the excesses of our Corinthian brothers and comparing what Paul describes here as an orderly meeting with what we have in most of our churches, I must admit that our idea of worship seems more like a celebration at the local mor- gue. Our concept of order comes from our cultural and religious background and has little to do with what we read in Scripture. If some Bible-believing, evangelical theologian was to make a study of meetings in the New Testament and honestly compare them to ours, we might come to realise just how unbiblical we really are.

Guidelines for receiving prophecy

Concerning handling prophecy in the church, I will conclude this chapter with ten guidelines. But first let me say that we are sometimes too idealistic when bringing or judging prophetic words. We expect them to have the same poetry and accuracy as those of Scripture, and so they are often brought with booming voice or in the antiquated English of the Authorised Version which may impress some people, but definitely not the Lord.

Obviously, when we prophesy, mistakes are made which we must not attribute to our heavenly Father. 'Thus says the Lord, er...I have forgotten thy name,' is not exactly going to be a great encouragement. However, the following word, brought by a simple soul who had been recently converted, did have the desired effect in spite of its apparent inconsistencies. 'The Lord says that there is someone here who is not well. I'm not exactly sure what the problem is, but if you come forward I think I can heal you!' Because we are called to judge and weigh, there must be room for experiment, and those who bring prophetic words should be open to receiving correction. The very fact that Scripture calls us to judge prophecy shows us that people who prophesy are vulnerable. Our security is in the body of Christ and our love and respect for one another.

Beware of outsiders who come into your church or fellowship and prophesy without first submitting to the leadership, and under no circumstances allow anyone room who demands that their message goes unchallenged. If hard words do come they should be tempered with the pain of having to bring them. Even Jesus wept over wicked Jerusalem, that hypocritical, harlot city who had forsaken her God for other lovers.

The following are my guidelines for handling prophecy and most of them can also be used when weighing words of knowledge or wisdom. It is not an exhaustive list, you may think of others:

1   Is there anything in the utterance which clearly conflicts with, or contradicts Scripture?

2   Is the person giving the prophecy known to be of good character and stable behaviour?

3   If the word is predictive, has it been, or can it be fulfilled? Obviously time is sometimes required to check this and it should be borne in mind that many words are conditional. Point 6 also applies here.

4   Is the one bringing the prophecy willing for it to be weighed, or is that person insisting on being the judge of the words?

5   While we are all responsible for weighing words, it is helpful to ask whether there is a positive witness in the hearts of two or three leaders or folk respected for assessing prophecies. Interpretations of a prophecy can differ and sometimes mislead. They should not be used with the word itself.

6   Are there, or have there been, any other confirmations? God will bring his word to pass; there is no need to strive.

7   Has the utterance benefitted the meeting generally or have any individuals been helped? It is well to remember that the fruit of the Spirit is love, joy, peace, etc, as opposed to envy, depression, conflict, and so on (see Galatians 5).

8   Does the person bringing the prophecy accept and submit to the recognised leadership of the group?

9   If the word is correcting direction set by the leadership, or critical of it in any way, has it been brought

privately to the leaders first?
10   Is the word manipulative?

Clearly one cannot go through such a checklist each time a prophetic word is given. A quick communication between those responsible for leading the meeting is usually enough. Where a word is plainly out of order some public acknowledgement should be made. 'Ums,' and 'ahs' and similar noises made to cover your embarrassment will not bring security to the flock. You need to lovingly let folk know that you are in control. Less serious or unharmful discrepancies can be dealt with, for the most part, after the meeting, if, indeed, it is necessary to deal with them at all. We don't correct every inappropriate prayer, hymn or even sermon for that matter. We tend to be extra sensitive in areas which are new to us and give little or no critical attention to those we are familiar with. Overall, I believe we are inclined to fight shy of loving confrontation. It is easy to justify letting things pass without comment on the basis that we don't wish to hurt. But we must remember that we have a responsibility to the whole gathering and need to ask ourselves who may be hurt if we ignore some harsh or unhelpful prophecies.

Having said all of this, our goal should always be to release and encourage the use of tongues, interpretation and prophecy at every level of church life. Properly used and monitored these gifts will glorify Jesus, strengthen, build up and enhance our gatherings and ministry and often lead to miracles of repentance and healing.

8

Spiritual understanding – wisdom, knowledge and discernment

Christine

The Holy Spirit's gifts are like a reservoir in the middle of a dry dusty plain. The banks are raised and the water is therefore just out of sight. It is possible to be close to the supply without ever realising it's there. The truth of this is evident when we see a powerless church seeking to meet the needs of a thirsty world. How intensely we pray for answers to people's problems and situations. We see their lives blighted and fruitless, like a garden after a long drought: the grass no longer green but brown, the flowers dried up and seemingly dead, the ground cracked and parched. On the other hand, God's resources are full to overflowing, lapping against the very edges, straining to be allowed to gush out over the dry, thirsty, gasping peoples of this world.

Perhaps this picture is not how you see it at all. You may be thinking that you are much more down to earth. What you see is the affluence in so many people's lives: the shiny new red car, excellent education, good homes, nutritious food. These can be just gaudy plastic flowers, covering over the real state of affairs: the desperate barrenness, the painful self-examination, the buried questions and the tears.

The gulf between the two pictures, one of dry desolation and the other of life-giving water, can be spanned by tapping into the Holy Spirit. His desire is to be a conduit between all that God wants to pour out and the desert places in our lives that cry out for his refreshment. The Bible promises that a time is coming when the Holy Spirit will be poured out on all humanity, but at this present moment we are not experiencing that indiscriminate, all embracing overflowing. The Holy Spirit is looking for people through whom to work. Continuing the water and reservoir analogy, through the church God is setting up an irrigation system by which he can potentially water and refresh the whole world. The particular gifts of wisdom, knowledge and discernment provide some of that life-sustaining, indeed life-inducing, water. Let's look at them in a little more detail.

The wisdom of God

Desire for the gift of wisdom for self-gratification got the whole human race into trouble. In Genesis 3:6 we read, 'When the woman saw that the fruit of the tree was...desirable for gaining wisdom, she took some and ate it.' Eve really got it wrong. Desiring wisdom to bolster your own pride is not what the Lord wants. He does, however, want us to use this precious gift.

Solomon, asked God for wisdom and knowledge. He could have asked for anything he wanted as the Lord said, 'Ask for whatever you want me to give you' (2 Chron 1:7). He didn't ask for wealth, honour, long life, the death of his enemies or health. Wisdom was his choice. The Lord threw in wealth, riches and honour.

This wisdom was apparent in Solomon's life in two distinct ways. Through his practical skills, which helped him to mastermind the building of the Temple and complete his writings, we observe a general flow of wisdom in his life. Every Christian should have a measure of this wisdom which comes from God. James instructs us if we lack wisdom to ask for it from the God who gives liberally (Jas 1:5).

Beyond this general wisdom, Solomon at times had a specific gift that was startling in its application. An example of this supernatural wisdom is found in 1 Kings 3:16–28. Two women shared a house and both had given birth to sons within a few days of one another. The first woman explained that the other's child died during the night while they were both sleeping. The second woman substituted the dead child for the living one. In the morning, when the first woman awoke, she found the dead child beside her. Examining it closely she saw that it was not her child, so she pressed the king to force the second woman to give up the live child. The second woman, however, insisted that it was her son.

Here indeed was a real dilemma. There was no way of actually knowing which woman the living child belonged to. Solomon could just have weighed the evidence and given a judgement, or he could have shrugged and said something about possession being nine-tenths of the law. He did neither. He reached into the supernatural wisdom of God and made his statement: 'Bring me a sword. Cut the living child in two and give half to one and half to the other.' He knew this would bring a good result. Immediately the true mother said, 'Please, my lord, give her the living baby.' She desperately wanted her son to live – even more than she wanted justice. The first woman said, in effect, 'Yes, that's fair, neither of us shall have a living son.' The gift of wisdom had revealed the true mother.

God could have given Solomon a word of knowledge,

but no one else would have had any means of judging what he said, for the women would have continued their argument. As it was, the truth was plain for all to see.

This wisdom is not a technique, for in another situation or in a different culture it would not have worked. We must always be alert and aware that what God blesses and uses one day will not automatically produce the same result in a similar situation. Like the manna which fell fresh in the wilderness each day, and stank if it was stored, we must continually draw on the Holy Spirit for each day's supply.

Solomon's renowned wisdom spread abroad. The fame of it even brought the Queen of Sheba to his palace. Isaiah 60:3 says, 'Nations will come to your light, and kings to the brightness of your dawn.' Surely this is the promise of an outcome similar to that which Solomon experienced. Can the Holy Spirit enlarge our vision sufficiently that we believe that with his wisdom flowing through us, his church will confound kings, queens and heads of state? Can we trust that the wisdom of the Holy Spirit will be so evidently displayed and show the way, rather like a lighthouse in a dangerous ocean, that people in high office will be drawn and directed by it? Our God is big enough; let's trust him to fulfil his own scriptures.

There is a difference between the world's view of wisdom and the wisdom of God. 1 Corinthians 3:18 sums it up: 'Do not deceive yourselves. If any one of you thinks he is wise by the standards of this age, he should become a "fool" so that he may become wise.' Because so much of our thinking and understanding have been conditioned by the world in which we live, we should constantly seek out and rely on the Holy Spirit's wisdom in order to unlock situations, discern the Enemy and protect the church.

The gift of wisdom can help to overcome our vested interest if we allow it. The mother of the living child in Solomon's court bent before the wisdom of God and relinquished her son. The other woman felt it was unjust that her child had died, so she resisted God. If she could not possess the live child, no one should. For her, it was all or nothing, her selfishness had prevailed.

A friend called John not only exercised wisdom, but he was prepared to lay down his personal desire, or child you might say, to see someone else's live. Let me explain. John was just about to leave his job to give all his time to pastoring a church. He was going to take most of the load from Norman, who was already doing the job and more, so Norman could concentrate fully on the growing missions work. It seemed like an excellent idea, but the Holy Spirit spoke to John and it was all change. The supernatural wisdom led in an altogether different direction, which cut right across his own interests. He told the church that they must not pay him a salary. Instead, he would continue to work and at the same time do more in the church. Young Peter was the man who should be paid and released to Norman as a full-time administrator. 'Young Peter' was not in the mix at this point; it was a real word of wisdom as time has shown. John was prepared to put his ambitions in God on a hold, in order to submit to the Holy Spirit and benefit Norman. In God's time John came into his ministry and now shoulders all the pastoral care for the church.

While writing these very pages, circumstances took me unexpectedly to a hotel in Brighton. I was sat in the lounge with two other ladies, one from Australia and the other from Thailand, and we prayed together. A couple of maids were circling around, dusting and cleaning. They were obviously coming as close as they dared, without actually disturbing us, so that they could listen in on our conversation with God. We took a break from praying and began to chat with the girls. They asked questions and we answered them. One of the girls explained that she was working in order to get money to help her through university. I suddenly felt the Holy Spirit prompt me and I said to her, 'You are faced with having to make a choice between two options which will take you on parallel courses. One is wise and the other very foolish.' I then told her what the outcome would be. The Lord had graciously given me a word of knowledge, which led on to a word of wisdom for that young lady. I was able to introduce her to a God who cared enough for her to give me, a perfect stranger, some supernatural advice for her situation.

Let me give you one further example of this gift in operation. The main hall of a growing church in the Thurrock area was bursting at the seams with people. Something obviously had to happen if the church was to continue to grow. The leaders met together to talk and pray. What could they do? Should they extend the building or look for a larger site? During the prayers one leader heard the Lord say, 'Do neither, plant out a whole section of the people.' A considerable number of folk had been travelling in from another area. They accepted the word, took action and the church grew on two fronts rather than one.

Words of knowledge

I looked up the word 'knowledge' in my *Oxford Dictionary*. Basically in English usage it means, 'a person's range of information, theoretical or practical, gained by experience'. That is not a definition of God's gift of knowledge, however. My own experience of using the word of knowledge is that I suddenly know something about which I have no information, no understanding and no experience. This can be a bit of a shock, not only to yourself but to the person or persons involved. The word of knowledge, then, is information about a person or an incident which could not possibly have been discovered from any source other that the Holy Spirit. I'll give you a couple of startling biblical examples.

In 1 Samuel 9 we read that Saul was looking for his father's donkeys. He just couldn't find them. He decided to visit the prophet Samuel to ask him about the animals. When Saul arrived at the town where Samuel was staying, before he could get the words out of his mouth Samuel told him the donkeys had been found. What's more, Samuel had a meal prepared for him. Samuel had received a word of knowledge the previous day and knew not only where the donkeys were but to order the meal from the kitchen in advance.

In John 1:47–51, Jesus greets a man called Nathanael, who immediately asks, 'How do you know me?' Jesus replies, 'I saw you while you were under the fig tree before Philip called you.' Jesus knew Nathanael before he had even come into view. How wonderful or awesome it is to realise that God sees us wherever we are; to know that our lives and circumstances are important enough to him to give knowledge to another person, simply for our encouragement. Heavenly knowledge is given not only to point out sin, or give direction, but also to strengthen and bless.

From time to time the Holy Spirit gives me a gift of knowledge. It really is very useful when you can't get to the bottom of a problem and the answer seems to evade you. Suddenly the Spirit moves and provides information which leads you to the root of the difficulty. Recently, some of us were praying with a young woman and although we felt the Spirit had shown us what we were dealing with, we weren't getting through. We sat back and I asked the Lord to help me to understand what was going on. Immediately I received a picture of this young lady as a baby, and I saw her mother having such bad post-natal depression that she was taken into hospital with a nervous breakdown. That was enough. I shared what I had seen and said, 'I think you have taken the blame for what happened to your mum and it's a lie, you are not responsible!' There was the surprised 'How did you know?' Once the explanations were over, we were able to set that girl completely free.

Another woman came to me in great distress on one

occasion. Her marriage was breaking up, her life had been a series of disasters. She knew where the problem stemmed from but she was totally unable to vocalise what it was. She really was incapable of speech. Every time she tried to talk about it, her throat closed up, her tongue stuck to the roof of her mouth and tears coursed down her cheeks. It was fairly obvious that she was demonised, but if I was to help this lady I needed to know what the root cause of the trouble was. I cried out to the Lord and the Holy Spirit caused images to tumble through my mind. They were so horrendous that I wanted to stop.

Before I could go any further I needed to gain reassurance from the Lord for myself. The images were too foul to vocalise, so I drew matchstick drawings. I showed the woman the first picture. She looked at it, then at me. She closed her eyes and huge tears squeezed out and ran down her cheeks. She nodded. So my mind wasn't playing tricks; the Lord was giving me supernatural knowledge. I drew more pictures and each one brought a nod, accompanied by many sobs and tears. Finally, no more pictures came. I took a deep breath and asked, 'Do you want to be free?' Emphatic nodding of the head gave me my answer. We went into the kitchen, and in the sink we burnt all the drawings. As they went up in smoke, the woman herself seemed to go through physical agony. I turned the taps on and all the ash was washed away into the sewer, the place where it belonged. She was free. She was able to speak, to pray, to ask for forgiveness and also to give it. It was all over. Before she left I gave her what I believe was a word of wisdom: 'Don't tell anyone else anything about today. Just live your new life to God's glory.' Before very long other members of her family were knocking on my door. They were amazed by the total change in her and were anxious to find out if God could do the same for them. We really do need the Holy Spirit today!

While at a large Christian conference, I needed to go

into a room to get something. There a young man in his
late teens was being counselled. As I was about to slip out
again the man in charge said, 'Christine, you don't have a
word here that might help? We really aren't getting any-
where at all.' I turned and looked at the teenager, and
found that I knew something. I said, 'Do you know
whether or not you were nearly hung by your own umbili-
cal cord at birth?' He turned to the woman sitting beside
him and said, 'Well, did that happen Mum?' His mother
confirmed that it was true and from there we were able to
deal with his suicide attempts.

The gift of discernment

1 Corinthians 12:10 speaks of 'the ability to distinguish
between spirits'. In the Amplified Bible the gift is
described as 'the ability to discern and distinguish between
the utterances of true spirits and false ones'. This definition
leaves us with a very black-and-white choice which is often
a cause of much pain. If a spirit is judged not to be the
Holy Spirit, the only alternative according to this definition
is that it must be a false or evil spirit, which is not always
the case. There is a third option – the human spirit, or better, soul. Much that is said and done, particularly in the
church, is not motivated by evil spirits directly, but by our
enthusiasm, ambition, sentiment, or the like. Of course,
such wrong motivation must be sensitively dealt with, but
to label it as being induced by evil spirits or false
prophecies is dangerous and damaging and will have bad
repercussions in the church or fellowship. If somebody
gave me £10 for every occasion I've acted in my own
strength or power, especially as a young believer, I might
be rich. Most of us, if we are honest, have done this not
only when prophesying or bringing words of knowledge,
but in preaching, praying and even counselling. Further,
not everything which comes from the human soul is bad for

even when we look at the world we see acts of kindness and goodwill expressed which we could not call evil.

The gift described in 1 Corinthians 12:10, when bestowed upon someone by the Holy Spirit, can help us to know and identify what kind of spirit we are dealing with, and the truth about what they may be saying. The gift should operate in counselling or ministry to folk who appear to be demonised, but equally in the church to protect the saints from manipulation and deception by evil spirits and well meaning human error. Certainly, different kinds of spirits are referred to in Scripture, and recognising them is a part of the gift of discernment. Evil spirits, unclean or foul spirits, spirits of infirmity, deaf or dumb spirits are all mentioned in connection with Jesus' ministry, but we need to take care. Although these demons can cause all kinds of sicknesses and problems, they also delight in pushing us into the ridiculous, and it is not unheard of for so-called exorcists to talk about spirits of nail-biting, nose-picking or even book-reading!

In the light of this, as with all the gifts we use, we need to accept responsibility for what we say so that we can be held accountable. We are not intended to go about dropping bombshells in public and making statements without facing the results of our words and actions. If we discern that someone is being troubled or manipulated by a particular spirit, and we claim to have dealt with it, then that person's life should be clearly turned around. If nothing is different we must be honest enough to say that either we got it wrong or that we were unable to do the job. We can, and do, make mistakes, which is why the Scriptures call for us to allow judgement and weighing of what is said and done. In this way, through relationships and submission within the body of Christ, we shall exercise the gift without causing damage to one another.

Sadly, some believe that they have 'discernment' when what they really have is the ability to be critical, and not always in the best possible way. All that disturbs them or that they disagree with is judged to be caused by an evil spirit. Others make subjective errors, feeling that all outward signs which have the appearance of evil are demonic. Thus screaming, frothing at the mouth, fits, and so on are all labelled demonic. If this were the case, why do we need the gift of discernment at all? People act in this way for many different reasons. For example, they may be physically ill, or psychologically disturbed and so we must not rely solely on human assessments on such occasions. Remember, too, that the gift of discernment will also uncover things at times when all seems outwardly peaceful, quiet and lovely. Because of the importance of this subject I shall be looking at the whole matter of demons and heavenly powers in more detail in Chapters 12 and 13.

We should treat very seriously the privilege of using the Holy Spirit's gifts. I have noticed that familiarity sometimes breeds contempt here. It is possible to become used to operating certain gifts and almost take it for granted that they are always there for the asking. The Amplified version of 1 Corinthians 12:4 says, 'Now there are distinctive varieties and distributions of endowments...and they vary, but the Holy Spirit remains the same.' From this scripture I understand that the Holy Spirit is totally trustworthy. It makes sense; God never changes. So the unpredictable element in every situation has to be you and me. Our spiritual condition makes the difference as to how the Holy Spirit functions through us and how successfully we achieve his desires. Relying on his presence with us is fine – we must do that – but taking for granted that he will use us in a specific way or when we are in pride or in poor heart, is dangerous. Without moving in fear or condemnation we do need to ensure that we keep humble and close to God lest we become the victims of the Enemy we seek to control. Each one of us can potentially be motivated by the Holy Spirit, by our own human spirit or by false spirits. It is vital that we do not slide through neglect of our relationship with the Lord from one realm of influence to another.

When the Holy Spirit is at work good things happen, lives are changed, situations are dealt with and blessings and judgements abound. When we are operating in our own spirit or even manipulated by unholy spirits, there may be fun and games, fascination and manifestations, but what is the fruit? I have observed folk casting out just about everything, including the kitchen sink; it is all very impressive but still something resists their every effort. The forces we battle with even enjoy the show themselves and know that they are sapping the strength and resources of the saints. If only here the Spirit of true discernment could be let loose, we might have to eat humble pie at times, but we would certainly get a lot more done in the long run.

Many of us have been in meetings where people go down under the power of the Spirit; even here some of us should ask the Holy Spirit for discernment as there are times when another spirit slips in and, among all the blessing, is engaged in the Enemy's work. In one such gathering I realised that a man had 'gone down' under some other power. I knelt beside him and gently asked him to stand up and continue seeking the Lord. I was convinced that God wanted to speak to him, and that an evil spirit wanted to stop that from happening. He persevered and God did speak. Over the next few months, with the Holy Spirit's help, he had to work out a few things in his life, but Jesus triumphed. Having a nice feeling in a meeting is no substitute for doing necessary business with God. So let us rely on, but never take for granted, the Holy Spirit and his wonderful, supernatural gifts.

Receiving the gifts

From time to time I'm asked how these gifts work through an individual and I have to say there is no neat set of rules, otherwise Scripture would give them. There is always a danger in telling folk your own experience as this can so easily present a psychological barrier. We must remember that the Holy Spirit will find his own way of revealing himself. Suffice it to say that our imagination needs to be redeemed and given over to the Lord. For too long Satan has had freedom to invade our beings through this doorway, hence the tremendous hold horoscopes and fortune telling have over so many people; they are just two of the devil's counterfeit gifts and cause some of us to be fearful of the real thing. When we yield this area of our imagination to the Spirit we will find that he may speak to us through words, pictures or strong impressions. These should be shared in a submissive and humble way and as we are shown to be right we will grow in confidence. (Guidelines for weighing words of wisdom, knowledge and discernment are similar to those at the end of Chapter 7, on judging prophecy.

The gift and the Giver

Following my mention of counterfeit gifts, I would like to touch on what might be a delicate point for some, but it needs to be addressed as there may be those who are left confused or in fear of their abilities. It concerns the function of gifts before and after conversion. The question is, do we use the same gifts we had before we came to Christ? If so, are we not in danger of bringing occult practices into the church if we were used in this way in our past? The Bible does not seem to be totally clear about this, which leaves an area of debate and concern. However, if we differentiate between ability and inspiration I believe we have the answer. An ability such as intuition or an active imagination can be under the control of the Holy Spirit or an evil spirit or simply used by the person themselves. So the ability is not of itself good or evil; it is where the inspiration comes from which is important. Most of us do not have a problem, for example, in the area of music or teaching, but our fears surface when it comes to the prophetic or revelatory areas. But why should these be any different as all abilities can be used for good or bad?

A certain friend led a church in London. On two separate occasions he saw women from the local spiritualist church soundly converted. They repented of their past involvement and renounced all connection to spiritualism and its practices. There was no doubt in his mind the break and deliverance in both cases was complete. One of these women clearly now operates a Holy Spirit-anointed gift of healing and the other words of knowledge – similar areas to the counterfeit gifts they had used previously. And what is more, these women have been going on with God consistently for between ten and twelve years.

This, and other experiences, has led me to see a distinction between an ability and the inspiration behind the function of that ability. When a Marxist orator comes to Jesus and turns himself over to the Lord. His inspirational preaching gift is the same one he operated before, but obviously now under a different anointing. The confusion may arise as a result of the Holy Spirit providing both gift and inspiration supernaturally at the same time, as he does on rare occasions, for example, when someone is anointed to sing or play an instrument way beyond any ability they possess. This would lead us to see the two things always as one and solely related to the inspiration. Therefore we would expect the ability as well as the inspiration to be lost when the source is taken away, but in normal circumstances this does not happen.

On the subject of counterfeit, it is helpful to know how they tackle the problem in the Bank of England. Those who are responsible for identifying forgeries are never given a false note to study, as this would only confuse them. Every batch of fraudulent notes will differ in some small way from another. Therefore, as no two are going to be the same, there is no point in spending time scrutinising them. In fact, the one who only examines counterfeits has no means of recognising the true, because while the copies have many features contained in the original, the checker has no yardstick, nothing to compare them with. So in the bank they are made to study the real thing until they know and recognise every minute detail. With this intimate knowledge they can then recognise even the tiniest deviation.

Some Christians become fascinated by the counterfeit, but the more they familiarise themselves with the bogus the less likely they are to know what reality looks like. When a supernatural manifestation or gift is not obviously unbiblical or morally twisted, the only way we can determine its origin or source is to resort to our knowledge of the truth. The closer our walk with Jesus, and the more intimate our relationship with the Holy Spirit, the more readily we will recognise what is not inspired by them. The reason I say this is because the best deception is closest to the genuine. Some false healing, words of knowledge, miracles, experiences of peace, joy and even pseudo-righteousness will appear to be almost exactly the same as the true. Without the Spirit's help we will fall into the trap of receiving them in our enthusiasm or, equally as bad, rejecting the genuine out of fear. Therefore, let us keep near to Jesus and those who love him.

In 1 Corinthians 12 Paul continually uses phrases such as 'to each one', 'to one', 'to another', 'distinctive varieties' and in verse 11, 'All these achievements and abilities are inspired and brought to pass by one and the same Holy Spirit, who apportions to each person individually exactly as He chooses' (AMPLIFIED BIBLE). This is not caprice, but all to do with God's purpose and our response. In the light of this, how important it is for us to work together with others, to blend our gifts, to uphold one another, to make up one another's deficiencies. I have found tremendous security and comfort in relating to others whose gifts are very different. Sometimes I am frustrated by the restrictions and limitations which this brings, but long term I would not want to move in any other way. This, surely, is what church and the body of Christ is all about.

You may not possess all three gifts I've been writing about, but when this combination does come together it's absolute dynamite. Jesus used all the Holy Spirit's gifts during his lifetime, apart from tongues and interpretation which were specially reserved for the church. What 'wisdom', when presented with the woman taken in adultery, to give the sinless one the right to cast the first stone. The only one with that qualification was left with her when everyone else had disappeared, and he sent her away to sin no more. What 'knowledge' when he said to the woman at the well, 'You are right when you say you have no husband. The fact is, you have had five husbands, and the man you now have is not your husband' (Jn 4:17–18). Thus a poor Samaritan harlot became the first evangelist. What 'discernment' when he proclaimed the crippled woman in the synagogue to be 'a daughter of Abraham, whom Satan has kept bound for eighteen long years' (Lk 13:16), and then went on to set her completely free.

We are now the body of Christ, his agents on the earth, and the church is his weapon against evil. Let us entreat the Holy Spirit to fill us and use us in any way he chooses. Let us advance together in his gifts and power so that the Enemy will be pushed back and severely routed on every side.

9

Gifts of power –

faith, miracles, healing

Christin

'It is by grace you have been saved, through faith.' The
words from Ephesians 2:8 are perhaps among the be
known in the Bible when it comes to faith. Are we the
with reference to the gifts of the Holy Spirit, speaking
this kind of faith, which is the right of all believers? I d
not believe so. Obviously, it is the Holy Spirit who brin
us to salvation through faith, but the 'gift of faith'
something quite separate. Let's begin by looking at th
faith which is common to us all as Christians.

The gift of faith

To believe in anything requires faith. Centuries ago, th
predominant belief was that the earth was flat. It seeme
quite understandable, quite logical; everyone could se
that for men, buildings, trees and plants to remai
upright, the earth had to be flat. Then along came rebe
who challenged the traditional thought, and with the

116

calculations and dialogue came to the conclusion that the earth was not flat at all but rounded. The discovery took faith to believe, as no one at that time could fly into the heavens to view the curve of the earth to prove the point.

Similarly, it takes faith to believe in creation when you can't see the God who created. However, from my perspective it takes a lot more faith to believe in a theory of evolution which depends on us appearing from nowhere at all, and yet millions of people do.

We all have faith of some kind, but by the Holy Spirit we can have the faith *of* God which gives us faith *in* God.

'Now faith is being sure of what we hope for and certain of what we do not see,' says Hebrews 11 as it explains faith in action through our forefathers. All God's children and family live by faith, whether alive before or after Jesus' death on the cross. In fact, 'without faith it is impossible to please God' (Heb 11:6). Faith leads us into grace and all of God's other blessings. What, then, is this particular gift of faith given by the Holy Spirit? The 'gift of faith' is a singular impartation of faith given in special circumstances to further God's work, encourage his people or bring down the Enemy. It is a one-off 'charism' of the Spirit which produces a visible, tangible result.

In our early days of ministry John and I were 'living by faith'. We had no church or organisation to support us and at times it was very hard. Our money came out of the blue, in little brown envelopes. Some came through direct ministry but not a lot. Christians were not usually very generous in those days. One morning I dressed the children, put them in the pram and took stock of all the food I would need to buy for the next few days. I then looked at the large, solitary ten-shilling note which was all I had and went down my list again, trying to limit it to the money available. It was an impossible task; I would just have to buy what I could until the money ran out and trust that it didn't happen too soon. So off we went shopping, with Jesus and a prayer.

This was before self-service, and you had to know just how much everything was before you bought. You couldn't walk along the shelves looking at items and adding up amounts. The sales assistant got your goods for you, packed them in your bag and you paid up. I ordered what I wanted, handed over my note, counted my change, put it in my purse and left. Outside the butcher's I decided to check my money again before going in and making my purchases. I must have counted the coins a dozen times. They still added up to ten shillings. I knew it couldn't happen but it just did. I still had the same amount at the greengrocer's, the baker's and the cobbler's, then the money ran out. Thirty years later I can't explain what happened but I know that God did it. I have actually dressed my children for shopping without any money in my purse, believing that something would happen before I left the house; there it was, that little brown envelope laying on the doormat. For some reason the envelope was always a brown one, never a white one.

My faith in God as our Provider was born, tried and tested during those difficult times for the Holy Spirit did not always grant such specific gifts of faith, although I was brought to a place of expectancy when it came to the food and housekeeping. It is very strange as I look back now how much I actually limited God and boxed him in, for I didn't have any faith for new clothes. I dressed from jumble sales and the second-hand shops and, in retrospect, my looks bore testimony!

Phil Vogel, a member of Team Spirit to whom John referred earlier, has an unusual gift of faith for houses. He was led to take Jesus' word in Matthew 19:29 literally: 'Everyone who has left houses...for my sake will receive a hundred times as much.' Phil had given up his own home for the Lord, so on the basis of this scripture he went on to claim the hundred which were promised. As he only needed one for himself, he's been quietly giving them away ever since. Over the years I've watched him pray for saints who needed property for their work and I can't recollect a time when those he prayed for did not receive.

After two years of being homeless we finally ended up crammed into John's widowed mother's house. We had believed that God would provide us with a home but there was no prospect of one. One day John said to me, with no reason to hope, 'Today I'm going to see the house,' and off he went in the car. I can't say I waited for him to come back with bated breath, in fact, I forgot what he said almost as soon as he had left. He was on his own this time. When he did return late that night, he flew into the house and said, 'I've seen it!' And he had. For twenty years our life and ministry centred on that place. Sure, we went through a testing time, believing God for the deposit, believing him for the mortgage and finally believing him for the money to get our furniture out of store but that word of faith, spoken into John's heart, carried us through.

Miracles – God's intervention

Miracles are explosions of God's power, which defy his normal laws of nature. It seems when miracles occur God puts the normal laws on hold and brings some higher law into play. Three words stand out in this connection: signs, wonders and miracles. Of course, there's overlap, but essentially 'signs' are prophetic, 'wonders' are confounding, 'miracles' are resolving, and the Lord works all three to confirm his word and stop people in their tracks. The Bible accounts leave us to fill in the details and colours, the expressions on people's faces, that swelling sound of voices filled with awe and excitement. The necessary facts are there but often only half the story. I love to use my imagination. Imagine the feeding of the five thousand: the outbreak of good-natured laughter when the boy offered his packed lunch, the buzz of conversation when his offering was accepted and the sudden silence while it was being blessed, and then the rising roar of sound as the food multiplied.

A friend, Wendy Heslop, lives in Durban, South Africa. She and her husband were sent by their church to work in the nearby black township. Wendy found that when she visited the place everything appalled her. The poverty, the dirt, the disease, the despair conspired to make her feel hopelessly inadequate. She knew she couldn't work there but did not know how to tell her husband who was clearly called to the task. She cried out to God, 'There isn't enough of anything, least of all myself.' The Lord answered her, 'Just be the drop Wendy and I'll be the ocean.' Wendy didn't understand. It was so difficult to believe God for sufficient to meet the overwhelming needs that she saw everywhere she turned.

The time came to visit the township with her husband. She hadn't yet had the courage to tell him the truth. Later, she'd do it later. She grabbed a couple of packets of soup from her kitchen shelf, a salve to her guilty conscience. They climbed into their van and drove out to the 'centre' – simply a mud hut larger than the rest. Wendy produced her soup and what happened next she can't explain. Perhaps Cynthia, the lady in charge, didn't hear her, or maybe she didn't realise how little soup the packets would make. Anyway, she shouted out in a loud voice, 'Soup everyone! Wendy's brought soup!'

People came from everywhere to have some soup. 'What shall I do?' Wendy asked John her husband. 'Can I find the thinnest people and give what little there is to them?' 'No,' he replied, 'don't be crazy, just give the soup to the first few people in the line.' Feeling terrible and wishing she'd not been so hasty, Wendy helped Cynthia begin to ladle out the soup. Later, in fact some hours later, she looked up and realised that the queue had come to an end. She then looked down, into the bowl. It held the same amount of soup as when she started. Putting her arms around Cynthia she wept. Her tears dropped on to the surface of the dark brown soup and she could see them floating there. Again she heard the Lord's voice, 'You be the drop and I'll be the ocean.' Wendy has worked happily in that situation ever since.

And that's not the only time we've heard of modern miracles of food multiplication. David Matthews, a long standing-friend and member of our team, was in Mexico some years ago to see the work of Father Rick Thomas, a Roman Catholic priest working among the 'dump people'. He had heard about the many occasions when God had stretched the food and he was curious. He said to a large Mexican lady who was ladling out the food, 'How do you know when the food has multiplied?' Without any hesitation she said, 'When my arm aches.'

A part of Jewish tradition is the recitation of God's great exploits on behalf of his people. Moses, in the wilderness, believed for water from the rock and it was so. He stretched out his arms and God parted the waters of the Red Sea. The people of Israel were a people who treasured their corporate history with God, as well as their individual stories. Sadly, many modern saints have no sense of history, which leaves us with no real identity. We in the church, like our forefathers and Jesus himself, should be following the same pattern; we are now grafted on to that Jewish root with everything that means. Our history should be both ancient and modern as we look back to Abraham, our father, and forward to Zion, our city. Without this sense of continuity we are rootless, shallow and currently irrelevant.

If we do not understand and embrace our past we cannot properly value our future. Strangely enough, exactly the opposite is true for the Jew; he must understand his future in Christ before he can fully appreciate his past. We must come to realise that it was also for us that God performed the miracles of the past. He knew that we were on the way, and because he is unchanging we can anticipate him doing similar things for us today, not as Jews but as the full-orbed church of Jesus Christ.

I believe that as we take on our true identity as God's holy nation, so the whole earth will see these explosions of his power, not only endorsing our uniqueness as individuals but also revealing the glory of a united people in a divided world. The signs, wonders and miracles which attend the godly nation far outweigh those which follow a single prophet, as our Old Testament history teaches. It's really exciting to see yourself as part of God's continuing family and nation. Yet the truth is that we are also individuals, and a nation is only as strong as each single member. We all must be filled with the Spirit, so that the Spirit may overflow from each one into the church and out into the world in which we live.

'Heal the sick'

Another wonderful gift with which to overflow is healing. Some would point out to us that the Corinthian passage which outlines the gifts, refers to 'gifts [plural] of healing' (1 Cor 12:9), as opposed to a singular endowment. They believe this means that healing is not imparted as a once and for all ability but rather as separate blessings for each occasion. Others say the verse indicates that the Spirit gives different abilities or power to heal different kinds of sicknesses. Then there are those who believe they have a general gift which seems to be with them in most of their ministry. Experiences differ and support all of these views although I do favour the idea that a fresh gift is given for each occasion.

There seem to be at least three specific ways mentioned in Scripture in which healing can operate. Two of these are found in James 5:13–16. In verse 14 the directive is given that if someone is sick, he should call the elders of the church to pray over him so that they can anoint him with oil. James goes on to say the prayer offered in faith will bring healing. This would apply to people who are so sick as to be housebound and therefore unable to get to the elders! They take the initiative and the elders respond by applying the oil and praying. This practice is for church members who acknowledge their leaders, not a general means open to anyone. However, the Lord clearly blesses those who use oil for anointing with prayers in all kinds of situations, although only once, when he sent out the twelve (Mk 6:13) did he suggest it be used in general ministry. He is much more concerned with prayers of faith than with formulas and procedures. Verse 16 of the same chapter appears to be directed towards the whole congregation. As we confess our sins to one another and repent, we are to pray for one another to be healed. These two means of grace need to be employed much more frequently in our churches and fellowships.

The third means occurs in Mark 16:18 and should be viewed very much as part of our evangelism: 'They will place their hands on sick people, and they will get well.' These words, which come at the very end of Mark's Gospel, are given in the context of a general commissioning to 'those who believe', as opposed to the specific sending of the twelve mentioned earlier. The Lord commands his disciples to 'go into all the world', and directs them towards the lost.

I am convinced that we will see much more success in the realm of healing when we use the gifts to touch the needy as Jesus did. In fact, it is my conviction that we should be much more open to use all the supernatural gifts as we move about in our daily round of work, rest and play. Operating the gifts should be part of our everyday experience and lifestyle; there is little in the New Testament to support their use in any other way. Personally, I find myself being stirred by the Holy Spirit to share his gifts on planes, in supermarkets, on the street and in all kinds of situations.

We Christians are paranoid about healing and often quite self-centred. After all, we have the promise of *eternal* health whatever else happens in this life! Healing is not our goal, Jesus is! And as my husband often reminds us, everyone for whom Jesus prayed died of something else! But let's pray for the sick and let's see folk healed, for it is all an evidence that the coming kingdom is already among us. When we see people in the world getting blessed, perhaps our faith will increase and some of our long-standing problems in the church will bite the dust. Surely everyone should be involved in some, if not all three of these provisions for healing the sick.

A testimony from an Ichthus team who were doing door-to-door work in south-east London illustrates the fact that the Lord will bless us as we pray for the sick in our evangelism. At one of the homes they called on quite regularly a seventy-two-year-old invalid was confined to a wheelchair. He was an atheist but one day announced, 'I ought to ask this Jesus into my life, oughtn't I?' The team members prayed with him and he immediately got up out of his wheelchair to put the kettle on for a cup of tea! 'Goodness me, what on earth have I done?' he exclaimed. This man became the talk of the area as he walked back and forth to the meetings, something which he has done for some years now. He was baptised by total immersion and had no problems going down into the water even at his age.

Jesus shows us a multitude of approaches and solutions when it comes to healing, but no set techniques. He told some people that their *faith* had healed them, yet when the father of the demonised boy said, 'I do believe, help me to overcome my unbelief,' he cast out the evil spirit anyway. The Lord also said that it was the disciples' lack of faith which hindered some people from being healed, and on other occasions he pronounced forgiveness of sins which brought release and healing. Sometimes he became angry and the spirits of infirmity fled and folk were healed, but time and time again we read that he was moved by 'compassion'. His great example was his love for, defence of, and motivation towards God's creation in man. He was filled with love and the Holy Spirit, relying on the Spirit's gifts to

minister to sick and suffering humanity. His compassion was
never passive but moved him into action. The Spirit
instructed him and sickness, death, demons, sin; and the
elements came under his calm authority. This power of
Jesus is increasingly at work today in the church around the
world.

I get a little concerned with the strong emphasis some
place on techniques. Inner healing, healing of the
memories and visualisation are all very much in vogue
and some people are certainly blessed and very definitely
helped. What is disturbing is the preoccupation with
these and the seeming belief that we can explain and pass
on our methods. Certainly we can learn, but in the end
the Spirit responds to faith, prayer and trust. It is dangerous to attempt to do what someone else does without
their spirituality and gift, as is seen in the story of the
sons of Sceva recorded in Acts 19. Something John and
I have observed over the years is that people who use the
gifts are not always the best at teaching their use. In this
respect we need continually to consult the Scriptures as
our guide; lengthy and complicated teachings which go
way beyond the word should be treated with extreme
caution.

John and I were recently in South Africa, visiting the
Transkei, one of the homelands. (You have already read in
Chapter 1 about the expanding church led by Joseph Kobo.)
As a meeting in the church closed, we were expected to pray
for the sick. People lined up in queues in front of us. I found
the whole thing extremely daunting. As I looked at my
queue I was struck by the number of children who had come
forward for prayer so, through the interpreter, I asked them
what was wrong. One after the other said they had
headaches. I had a brainwave. Pointing to some drawings
and printed letters at the back of the church I asked how
many could tell me what they were. They couldn't see them
clearly at all; they needed glasses! So there was the answer –

glasses. If we could get them to the optician, all would be well. A little voice inside me said, 'Christine, what optician?' 'Whoops, sorry Lord, there aren't any, but they need glasses', I'm telling the Lord. 'What glasses, where, and with whose money?' seemed to come back the reply, as the sound of others praying increased. I can be thick on some occasions, but not this time. There were no opticians, no glasses, no money to pay for them; prayer was the only option left. I prayed and then asked the children again to tell me if they could see the pictures on the wall. Wide grins. 'Yes,' came back the answer in Xhosa. God had done the healing, not I.

One year at Spring Harvest a couple asked me to pray for their child who was almost totally deaf. He had terrible infections in his ears which, over a period of years, had almost destroyed his hearing. I admit freely that my faith was very low, but I prayed on the basis of the parents' faith. Some months later I received a letter telling me that from the time I had prayed, the child's hearing steadily got better until doctors confirmed it was perfect.

Those with young children know how they can plummet dramatically from health to sickness very quickly. This is exactly what happened one day with our son Matthew. I didn't worry initially, but suddenly I realised he was extremely unwell. Noel, our doctor, came very quickly and after examining him said, 'I think you should get John home from work. Matthew is really very ill indeed, he has viral pneumonia.'

Noel is a Christian, and after praying with us he left, saying he would come back later. I called John, gave him the facts and waited for him to return home. During that time, I went through a crisis with the Lord. I questioned everything I could possibly question, from why this was happening to whether God truly loved me, or I him. I finally came to rest and could honestly say with Job, 'The Lord gave and the Lord has taken away; may the name of the Lord be praised'

(Job 1:21). Before John arrived home he went through an experience similar to mine. Noel returned and told us that as a doctor there wasn't anything he could do for Matthew. He felt it was far better for him to be at home, with us, than alone in hospital. He then left saying that he and his wife would be praying for us through the night, and should we want him we only had to ring, he would be up. We had already decided to pray and fast and we put Matthew into our bed and lay down with him. In the early hours of the morning we thought the end had come. He became very still, sighed deeply and went to sleep. The next morning, he woke full of life and asked, 'Why am I in Mummy's bed? Can I go in the garden now?' We didn't know what to do, whether to laugh or cry. God had healed him. On Matthew's record Noel wrote, 'A miracle occurred.' Who can fathom the depths and power of our Saviour's love?

We have mentioned our South African friend, Joseph, several times. While we were visiting him in Transkei, he introduced us to the local chief and his wife, and finally, with great reluctance, told us their story in full.

When Joseph returned to his village as pastor, the chief was obviously out of his mind and clearly demonised. Some of the women had been praying for God to move, and one of the first signs that their prayers had been answered was that the chief experienced an amazing deliverance. This brought about his conversion and a mini-revival began. Some time later the chief's wife, who was pregnant with twins, went into labour prematurely. It was the rainy season and travel to get medical help was impossible. As she struggled to give birth it became evident that something was badly wrong. The twins had died in her womb and were decomposing. As she bled to death the stench was vile.

After eleven hours, they carried her corpse into the church meeting, and laid it on the platform. Joseph's mother-in-law, one of the great pray-ers among the women, was standing beside him. She dug him in the ribs, pointed to the dead woman and said, 'Pray!' As Joseph says, 'When your mother-in-law tells you to pray you do it!' He confessed to us that his faith level was at zero. He prayed the shortest prayer possible, and to this day cannot remember what he said. He then turned his back on the body and was just about to explain to his congregation that God didn't always raise the dead when he saw from their faces that something had happened. Their eyes came out like organ stops, and they started dancing and praising the Lord. He looked over his shoulder and there was the chief's wife, sitting, then standing up, alive and healed. From this one incident seven new churches were born. Our God brings life out of death and if he can do it in Africa he can do it in Britain too, Hallelujah!

Jesus the Healer is looking for us to co-operate with him. Better to pray fifty times and see only five answers than not to pray and have no failures. Smith Wigglesworth, well known for his healing ministry in the Pentecostal awakening earlier this century, said, 'If I pray for ninety-nine people and they all drop dead, I'll go on to pray for the hundredth.' Live dangerously, and don't be afraid of making mistakes. Unlike some Christians, I find that my neighbours are thrilled that I care enough to pray, even if they don't get healed. To understand just how dangerous silence and inactivity can be, read Matthew 25:14–30. From this parable of the talents I gain great encouragement. It seems that God isn't greatly concerned with our getting it right but is angered by us doing nothing.

We are promised in the Book of Revelation that a kingdom is coming where sickness, death, division, pain, poverty and hunger don't exist. Until that wonderful day is fully here we need to be a people who, by faith, stretch out to pull great chunks of it into the present. Jesus plainly taught that the kingdom of heaven is at hand. The evidence was, and still is, that the dead are being raised, demons expelled, the sick healed and the hungry fed. Jesus did all of those things and we, as his disciples, are challenged to be like the Master. Mind boggling though it may be, we must acknowledge that Jesus returned to his Father in order that the Holy Spirit might come to give us the wherewithal to follow in his footsteps. We must get our feet where Jesus put his – on the very head of Satan. We too must crush Satan by faith, miracles and healings which visibly demonstrate the fact that Jesus has already won the final victory.

10

By one Spirit into one body

John

The Holy Spirit is in the business of doing the impossible. He delights to do for us what we cannot do for ourselves. All he asks of us is trust and faith. That is why I
hold firm to the belief that we will see a united church
before Jesus comes back. With all the centuries and history of divisions there seems to be nothing more unlikely
and unattainable than unity among Christians. What a
tremendous opportunity for the Holy Spirit to work and
prove the spiritual pessimists wrong. Millions of sincere
Christians have absolutely no real hope for reconciliation
in the church this side of 'kingdom come'. Of course, I'm
not suggesting that the whole of the apostate church with
its systems and structures, together with all those who
remotely claim to be Christians, will be brought to unity.
Nevertheless, I have a deep, unshakable conviction that
a huge, remnant church will manifest a visible and recognisable unity to all peoples throughout the earth. Is there
scripture to support this? Definitely! Let's look at things
from a biblical perspective.

130

One nation under one King

First, let us go back to Ezekiel, the prophet of the Holy Spirit. His vision of a valley of dry bones, in Ezekiel 37, is a familiar one and speaks directly to this situation. God's people were dead. Their bleached bones lay white and parched in that eerie desert place. 'Can these bones live?' the Lord asks the prophet. I love Ezekiel's reply – how different it is to the cynicism we hear from the lips of many Christians today. 'No chance' from the house churches. 'Extremely unlikely' from the Anglicans and 'Don't talk wet' from the Baptists. But the prophet says, 'O Sovereign Lord, you alone know.' Then the Lord commanded him to prophesy, first, to the bones to come together and then to the breath to put life into those rebuilt corpses. After this he was given four great promises: 'I will put my Spirit in you', 'You will live', 'I will settle you in your own land' and 'You will know that I the Lord have spoken, and have done it.' Finally, through the miraculous joining of two sticks, we hear the divine proclamation that these once dead, divided and scattered people will again become one nation under one King.

I'll not argue with those who get excited about a literal fulfilment of these scriptures in natural Israel. It is amazing to see what God is doing with his proud, spiritually dead people in that little piece of land in the Middle East. I rejoice and claim Paul's promise in Romans 11:26 that 'all Israel will be saved', but saved to what? To reclaim a small piece of earth, to rebuild an ancient stone temple and reintroduce a law and animal sacrifices which can save no one? No, never! Read the rest of Romans 11 and chapters 9 and 10. Israel's destiny is to become one with all the redeemed and to inherit all the promises given through Christ's death and resurrection. The whole earth, not just a tiny square, is now theirs and ours in Jesus, and will be 'filled with the knowledge of the glory of the Lord, as the waters cover the sea' (Hab 2:14). We must not go back to an Old Covenant but on into the fullness of the New.

Jesus made it clear to those faithless, unrepentant, religious hypocrites who were supposed to be Israel's leaders that he was taking the Kingdom away from them and giving it to a people who would produce its fruit (Mt 21:43). Today we look for higher fulfilment of the Old Covenant promises in our future with Christ, not in a return to the past with our fathers. The old is a shadow, the new is the reality. That which is natural is first, that which is spiritual is second (1 Cor 15:46). Now we are Abraham's heavenly seed and will occupy, not just an earthly Jerusalem, but the heavenly city for which he had always looked and hoped (Heb 11:10).

So, then, Ezekiel's vision has a higher fulfilment in God's spiritual people and therefore tremendous relevance to us right here and now. Like the prophet, we are called to agree with God and accept his view about our future; our faith must not be eroded by the sight of our present tragic circumstances. We must prophesy encouragement and hope into the saints and also 'prophesy to the breath', or the Holy Spirit, to blow upon them. We must call Christians everywhere to come together in trust and to respect one another without compromising the distinctives which God has given. We must also pray for the Holy Spirit to fill not just individual Christians but whole gatherings and congregations as he did over and over again in the Acts of the Apostles.

This is exactly what we are beginning to witness among open, flexible Christians in every nation and from every tradition. This massive wave of God's blessing cannot be stopped any more than we could hope to hinder a tidal wave. God will have his way, the Sovereign Lord will accomplish it. Larry Christenson, a North American Lutheran charismatic, known all over the world for his ministry and writings, has said:

No other movement in the history of Christianity has ever spread so fast and so far.... Along with other Christians, charismatics have a major concern for Bible-centred, Christ-centred evangelization. But unlike any other group, they are the stream that goes everywhere...they are the only movement that involves Christians in all denominations and on every continent.

Only the Holy Spirit can do this. We must not be put off by the difficulties and problems, for they are many. When I first read Ezekiel 37 I missed one important factor – the rattling! I 'failed to realise that when dead bones are brought to life and seek to find their place, there's a dreadful clatter. I expected all to be peaceful and orderly, and for a time was quite disillusioned until I realised that there is a price to pay for unity. It will take time and commitment, patience and love but we will be victorious. I have more good scriptural reasons for believing this: look at John 17.

Jesus' prayer for unity

In this chapter we see what should truly be called the 'Lord's prayer'. The earlier prayer Jesus taught his disciples to pray is really our prayer; it's the one he gave to his followers. In this passage we find Jesus praying for the unity of his disciples and all who believe. His reason was, 'so that the world may believe' and understand (vv 20–23). Do you believe that our heavenly Father is a prayer-answering God? I guess you do, but do you want to qualify this by saying that he responds to faith? OK then, do you believe that Jesus prayed in faith? Surely none of us would reply to this in the negative. Let me ask one further question: Whose prayers above all others' does the Father delight to answer? Obviously his Son's prayers have a special place in his heart and are high on his agenda, so we can be absolutely sure that the most important prayer ever uttered in history, by the One most beloved of the Father in any age, will be answered in its entirety! The Holy Spirit will not rest until this goal is achieved.

Sometimes it's difficult to hang on to this when you're going through relational traumas. As a Christian, I was born with a vision of a restored, powerful church and sang those early songs with faith and enthusiasm: 'We are being built into a temple', 'Thou dost seek a bride all pure and holy', 'Behold how good and pleasant it is', 'God looks for a people', 'The promised land God gave us' and many more. In fact, the majority of the choruses and songs on the church and unity around that time actually sprang from musicians related to the stream of which I was part. The fellowship which started in our home in the mid-sixties grew in numbers and talent until, in many ways, we were at the forefront of what God was doing creatively in the church during those years. A few of us drafted a handwritten leaflet with our first names on it and invited our friends to the Albert Hall to 'praise God together'. It was packed to the doors. Miracles, wonderful ministry, talented actors and dancers all came together and we were on the crest of a wave. I could only believe we would go on from strength to strength, but I had sadly underestimated the power of the Enemy to exploit our weaknesses.

I remember often preaching during those days and asking such questions as, 'Should all this fail and fall apart at the seams, would we give up, or would we pick up the pieces and go on with God?' and 'Does the revelation change with our circumstances or does the truth stand firm whatever is happening around us?' My personal responses were sincere and, as best I could, I had counted the cost, but I honestly couldn't see my faith being tested so soon and so sharply. We had been through so much together – all the laughter and the tears, the giving and receiving. But division came; friends moved away from us. I wept; I prayed; I reasoned; I forgave; I lay awake night after night and still, after seven or eight years, the ache is there and there is much that I just do not understand. But the Holy Spirit lovingly and tenderly brought my words back to me and they became a foundation of faith on which I could rebuild my life. Today I am as convinced as ever that Jesus' words are true: 'I will build my church, and the gates of hell will not overcome it' (Mt 16:18).

In reality, the fellowships around us have never fully recovered from that time of division. Lots of good things continue to happen and many people have been blessed and helped but something was finished. Like a tree that had been broken off at the root, I watched the majestic branches dry up and wither. But now, taking my attention away from the tree which had held such promise and looking back to the stump, I see healthy new growth and know that God has not given up on us yet. In the meantime, there is also a fresh and exciting movement of the Spirit blowing through more and more of the traditional churches. Many of the truths we struggled to bring to light, and were widely criticised for, are now just as widely accepted and it seems we have been joined (or overtaken?) by an army of others who are just as determined to press on into all that the Lord has for his people.

What is even more thrilling is that many other pioneers of renewal and restoration, having been through their own experiences of success and failure, are joining hands to support one another. The tide of blessing truly is rising both in the UK and worldwide as networking is beginning to take place, not through man-made structures but through relationships of love. It appears that whenever Satan seeks to destroy what God is doing, the seeds of life are spread and he is worse off than before. In God's kingdom-economy, death always produces life and Satan ultimately works the purposes of God. He just can't win.

'The unity of the Spirit'

The mystical army which Ezekiel saw, and which is being raised up by the Spirit, is the army of the Lord. This means that its soldiers are under his command and will, therefore work in relationship with one another. Submission to the lordship of Jesus, and mutual submission within Christ's body based on love, trust and recognition, are inseparable. John, in his first letter, says, 'If anyone says, "I love God," yet hates his brother, he is a liar' (1 Jn 4:20). Paul says in Ephesians 5:21, 'Submit to one another out of reverence for Christ.' No divine army, reflecting the nature of the God it serves, can function without love and submission, and it is the Holy Spirit, the Spirit of unity, who will help us to do what we cannot do ourselves.

In Ephesians 4:3 we are urged, 'Make every effort to keep the unity of the Spirit through the bond of peace. There is one body and one Spirit....' From this we learn that all striving to achieve unity is futile. While we continually struggle to obtain unity we are failing to acknowledge that we already possess it. Unity is the free gift of the Spirit to every believer who enters, or is baptised, into the body of Christ. I am now one in Christ with every other true believer in the world. I can seek to build on that reality or to destroy it, but if I destroy it I destroy myself. Paul clearly warns us of this in his instructions in 1 Corinthians 11:29–30 concerning eating the Lord's Supper together: 'For anyone who eats and drinks without recognising the body of the Lord eats and drinks judgment on himself. That is why many among you are weak and sick, and a number of you have fallen asleep [or died].' Stern words, but completely understandable if we really believe that we are one body. If I hate you or hurt you, I hurt myself, and more tragic still, I hurt my Lord for he too feels pain in his body.

Evangelical and charismatic Christians have not grasped this truth for one reason: we are individualists. We are brought up on a diet of personal salvation, a personal experience of the Holy Spirit and a personal walk with God. We can join and leave churches or relationships with other Christians almost as easily as we leave a job or our worldly companions. We have no sense of the corporate nature of the church. On the other hand, the people of Israel were so taken up with their corporate identity as the people of God that they frequently forgot about personal holiness. When Jesus came to the Jews, the leaders of the nation were so far away from God in their hearts that he uttered the most shattering words a Jewish priest could hear: 'You belong to your father, the devil' (Jn 8:44). No wonder they hated Jesus.

If we are to be effective as the army of God we must get this matter of our national identity sorted out. Salvation starts with a personal experience but it relates us to a family and ends with one nation under God. It's true that Jesus loves me and died for me, but he also loves his church and gave himself for her as well. He is not coming back for a lot of rugged individualists, doing their own thing, in their own way, for their own spiritual satisfaction. He's coming back for a nation – a nation of households, of families and tribes, all inter-related and working together under one King to accomplish one objective. And by now it must be obvious I'm not talking about organisational or institutional unity. The unity which the Spirit gives is a living, organic unity maintained by genuine love and honesty.

Looking back to Ephesians 4, we are commanded to 'keep the unity of the Spirit' (v 3), 'until we all reach unity in the faith and in the knowledge of the Son of God' (v 13), In between, as we saw in a previous chapter, we are given apostles, prophets, evangelists, pastors and teachers as the means of achieving the unity of faith and knowledge. We need help to make the transition from unity of spirit to unity of faith, and Jesus has provided it. How important it is, therefore, to seek out these ministries and encourage them to serve us in this respect. Many of them are already at work functioning both inside and outside of our denominations. They are helping us to build strong churches, encouraging those churches to relate together across the streams and pointing them all to the unfinished task of reaching the world in our generation. This is a key function of the primary apostolic ministry.

We cannot do this alone. No denomination, stream or even national church has a monopoly on truth or on the Spirit of truth. No one organisation or network has the resources required to reach every people group on earth. For even if we possessed unlimited spiritual power, we would be limited by our physical presence. We simply can't be everywhere all of the time. We desperately need one another. We need one another's encouragement and we need the discipline which our relationships bring. We need one another's skills and one another's resources, as well as all the rich cultural diversity which each people can contribute. We have spent centuries trying to get home by taking short cuts, but there really is only one way forward – together! The prophetic words of Ronnie Wilson's hymn, written over a decade ago, will mock those of us who sing them unless we continue to accept the challenge and remember – only the Holy Spirit can do this.

A body now prepared by God and ready for war,
The prompting of the Spirit is our word of command;
We rise, a mighty army, at the bidding of the Lord,
The devils see and fear, for their time is at hand.
And children of the Lord hear our commission;
That we should love and serve our God as one.
The Spirit won't be hindered by division
In the perfect work that Jesus has begun.

Ronnie Wilson © Thank You Music 1978

11

Out of the Upper Room

John

It was the 2nd October 1982. Cardinal Suenens was speaking at the third in an extraordinary series of celebration meetings. They were a joint effort arranged by leaders from within the Catholic renewal and the house churches, held in the Methodist Central Hall, Westminster. The other speaker that evening was Douglas McBain, a respected Baptist preacher well known in the renewal movement. The Cardinal spoke very clearly, and simply and I have never forgotten what he said: The essence of his message can be summed in one sentence: 'The renewal must get out of the Upper Room and on to the streets, or it will die!'

That word was of particular relevance to me as I came from a Salvation Army background and heard direct from my grandparents on both sides of our family how blessing spread when the gospel was taken into the open air in word, works and wonders. Marching, singing, flags, drama, comedy, praying, preaching and miracles were very much part of the Army's witness. Conversions frequently took place on the streets, and it was not uncommon to see drunkards become sober in a moment as they knelt around the drum which was used as a makeshift 'mercy seat'. Women worked alongside men as evangelists and faced the out-and-out aggression of the skeleton army with its 'skull and cross-bones' banners. These 'terrorists' deliberately organised attacks intended to stamp out the amazing work of the Holy Spirit which was taking place through Booth and his soldiers.

Until quite recently, the Army seemed to be losing much of the 'blood and fire' side of its ministry, concentrating more and more on the social aspects of its work. The 'works' were taking over from the 'word and wonders'. Physical needs seemed to take pre-eminence over those of soul and spirit, although happily there are signs that this trend is turning around. Some time ago the Pentecostals picked up the baton and were soon sidelined by the mainline denominations, but the movement fast became respectable and lost its radical cutting edge. Liberalism and declining attendance really began to weaken the historic churches immediately after World War II, and evangelicals were driven on to the defensive. They put the 'word' firmly back into the pulpit, outlawed 'wonders' as relevant only to the church's inception, and 'works' as social gospel akin to humanism. The scene was set for the rise of a new breed of Christians hungry for something to fill the spiritual vacuum in their lives. Against this background the house-church movement and the Charismatic renewal emerged, full of hope, enthusiasm and the Holy Spirit. However, if Satan can't stop you from following the Lord, he'll try to make you run before God.

Satan's strategy

Just as the strengths of the Salvationists, Pentecostals and the evangelicals became their weaknesses, so this is also a real danger for new church and charismatic Christians. The main emphases which have come through the most recent movements of the Spirit are first, the restoration of freedom and creativity in worship; second, the availability of spiritual gifts to all believers; third, the wider recognition of the apostolic and prophetic ministries; fourth, a fresh understanding of church and relationships; and fifth, a new vision of the kingdom of God in the here and now.

The Enemy does not panic when he sees that it is impossible to halt this wave of revelation and blessing which is running through the church. Rather, he strategises. 'OK, let them have a ball with their gifts but encourage them to use them on themselves. Keep it within the Christian ghetto.' He reasons, 'Relationships? Fine, let them love one another to death, then their precious relationships will turn sour! As for the kingdom, tell 'em that they are the kingdom and there's no one else quite like them, and pride will have 'em beat before they get started.'

Satan will do anything he can to hinder the church from achieving her commission. He seldom uses out-and-out confrontation, except where all else fails; he's too subtle for that. He's much more likely to encourage us for a while as an angel of light, so that we get used to his voice and presence. Then he gently adjusts the steering a degree or two and soon we're miles off course without even realising what he's done. He is fully aware there is no way he can stop the new army of enthusiastic, Spirit-filled saints from receiving fresh light and understanding. So he quietly and secretly moves within our midst to disrupt or, at least, contain things. He works on someone's pride or another's fear and slowly but surely sees that we get bogged down in ego trips, introversion or even just necessary maintenance. He's been at it for years, but thank God that the Holy Spirit is not naïve. He is constantly searching for humble, listening and pliable followers and will work with anyone who complies with his qualifications.

Marching for Jesus

It is very interesting to me to see what has been happening

since Cardinal Suenens made his prophetic statement. Graham Kendrick wrote his great marching song, 'Make Way', and at the same time the whole idea of marching and taking our worship on to the streets began to develop. Gerald Coates, Lynn Green and Roger Forster called us to march and pray through the streets of London in 1987. They were amazed at the response as 15,000 turned out that first year, around 60,000 joined them the next, and more than 200,000 went on local area marches in 1989. Who knows where this will end as they encourage us to 'march for Jesus where we are' in the towns and villages of Britain, and soon possibly in all the major cities of Europe. The church is on the move again. We are breaking out and taking our worship, praise and love for Jesus on to the streets once more.

Making Jesus known

We are also in the midst of a renewal of our vision for world evangelism. But let us not feel we are alone in this or that we are pioneers. Many in the Third World take this as a matter of course and have been doing so for years. Let me quote from a letter I recently received from Zimbabwe.

May I tell you about my gospel team of six young talented people with mixed extra-ordinary performances. They include high quality male voices and mixed music from the gospel. One other wonderful action by one young man is 'escapology' – escaping from the flames of fire. He wears sackcloth and we pour some paraffin over him but fire consumes the sackcloth whilst he remains unburnt. These dramas draw thousands of spectators as we win them for Christ. One action that has surprised many dentists is weight-lifting done by a young man using his teeth (see him in action carrying a 150 kg iron bar with his teeth from enclosed newspaper clipping). That is a railroad iron bar weighing 150 kg. He can dance still holding it with his mouth. The never boring music with ever boiling testimonies and sermons by the team have done much for God. Should we get sponsors over there we would pay you a visit and you would not let us leave your country!

The most arresting sight in the open air – even more than thousands of marchers – is the performance of a miracle of God's power. Some may have difficulty justifying biblically the activities of my beloved Zimbabwean friends, but surely we have no such problems with miracles. Jesus, our Leader, marched through all the cities of Israel with his followers doing wonders on the streets. He raised the dead, healed the sick, fed the five thousand and cast out demons and, as if that's not enough, as soon as the church got under way his followers carried on the work. Perhaps our reason for being so loath to take Jesus out on to the streets is that we believe 'our Jesus' is not as powerful as the one we see in the New Testament. Maybe we are embarrassed to put him on display, convinced that the world will be disappointed and let down by what he has to offer them.

This was not the case for one of the Ichthus network teams working in London. The team members started their open-air meeting by singing choruses. A few people gathered, including a local man who had been suffering from multiple sclerosis for five years. He was an avid music fan who had lived a life of petty crime, gambling and alcoholism but who was now confined to his wheelchair. He heard about Jesus from two on the team and indicated his desire to repent and make a heart commitment. So, right there on the street he received the Lord and was baptised in the Holy Spirit. Over the next two or three weeks workers called round to study the Bible and pray with him. Each time his health improved until he was walking long distances and had no further use for his wheelchair.

This is only one of a number of such occurrences of which I have heard. Some few years ago in the Midlands there was a similar case. A man walked out of his wheelchair in a shopping area. Most of his family immediately came to Christ and a report in the local newspaper brought many others into the kingdom. God still works today!

In my early days of ministry I spent much time in the open air preaching and praying for people with my colleague Norman Barnes and others. We had no difficulty drawing the crowds and constantly saw numbers of people make decisions to follow Christ. Not infrequently we saw folk healed, most notably a man with a paralysed arm while we were ministering in Charing Cross Road, London, one Saturday evening.

There was opposition too. Once we were preaching on Brighton beach and found ourselves in the middle of a group of hippies. They were painting a giant picture of Jayne Mansfield, the Hollywood sex goddess who had been killed in a car crash, using a large can of blue gloss house paint. I was protecting the speaker, a fiery Pentecostal brother named Bernard Tovell, who was going great guns on the stand while some youngsters were lighting matches under his coat tails. Right there God spoke to me in the midst of all that chaos: 'Can I have your suit son?' 'Of course, Lord,' I answered without thinking that it was the only one I possessed. Within seconds the leader of the hippies picked up the pot of paint in a fit of frustrated anger and hurled it at Bernard. He missed. The upturned can fell on my head and the paint trickled down my neck, seeping into every single article of clothing I was wearing. A great sense of peace and joy welled up within me. This was the first time I had experienced the Lord accepting an offering from me with such speed and clarity. Up to that time giving things to God had been a bit of an uncertain affair; I never really knew whether he'd taken them or not. Folk standing round urged me to press charges with the police who were quickly on the scene, but I found only love in my heart for those young people. The word went forth in power that day and hundreds gathered to hear it. I know the Lord can still move in power in the open air today. Why, then, did we stop that work?

The truth of the matter is that we were quite immature our-selves and not equipped to bring our converts into fellow-ship. So we redirected our efforts and energies into building strong churches and encouraging Christians everywhere to be filled with the Spirit and go deeper with the Lord. Today things have changed and, although the church is thinner and leaner, she is also fitter.

The decline in church membership continues but the churches which survive are, in the main, stronger. Many buildings have closed, but hundreds of new churches, mostly with no premises of their own, have sprung up. Although 'on paper' membership in many churches has not increased, numbers attending live churches have gone up. People are not now as concerned with the denominational tag as the quality of the life. In any thriving church, be it traditional or new, people are drawn from a wide variety of Christian backgrounds. The sheep are gathering where the food is and almost every city, town and even many villages boast one or more growing churches with a heart, a purpose and a wel-come. This I believe, is a work of the Holy Spirit and a prep-aration for an explosion of growth as the power and presence of Jesus is visible among his people once again. The time has come for the saints to rise up and get back out on to the streets again. We must take our joy, our message, our love and our miracles to the multitudes of ordinary people who are wait-ing to see the reality of Christ in us; they are not concerned with the external trappings of divided institutionalism.

Years ago, Graham Perrins, a friend from the earliest days of the house church movement, had a somewhat embarras-sing experience with the Holy Spirit. He came from a Breth-ren background, and after he had been baptised with the Spirit he took great delight in going around the churches challenging them with his new-found revelation. He was a skilled Bible teacher and revelled in painting a graphic pic-ture of what took place in the Upper Room. He spoke of the wind and the fire and the glorious chaos as the 120 disciples were suddenly smitten and filled with the power of God. He described the awe and pandemonium as each one began to speak in tongues which were totally foreign to them. He described the joy, the apprehension, the ecstasy, the laughter and the tears. At the peak of his tirade he would cry out and ask his hearers. 'How comfortable would you feel if this Upper Room experience were to descend into your respectable little fellowship this morning?' Of course, there was no answer to that and the majority did not even feel comfortable with Graham's challenge, let alone the thought of holy disarray in the meeting! Needless to say Graham's preaching opportunities declined.

Then one day, as he was praying in his study, he found himself face to face with the Lord, and the Lord was doing the talking. He certainly turned the tables on Graham by taking him back into the Upper Room where the disciples were enjoying the new wine. He showed him that there came a moment in the proceedings when the heavenly Bartender shouted, 'Time gentlemen please.' He then opened the doors and turned the disciples out into the marketplace at nine o'clock in the morning, still reeling under the influence of the Spirit they had imbibed. An equally pictorially vivid explanation of what took place outdoors followed as the crowds ran to see what was happening. The promise of the Spirit had come; there was shouting and crying and leaping and dancing and finally the accusation, 'These men are drunk!' 'Now,' said the Lord to Graham, 'How comfortable would you be if this were you and your fellowship outside Cardiff Arms Park on a Saturday after the big match?' Graham got the point.

Can we go on and on indulging ourselves in the Pentecostal outpouring and not share our joys without them going stale? I think not. The pool must have an outlet if the waters are not to become stagnant and polluted. Thank God for the March for Jesus, but let us not be fooled into believing that, because we are having our annual excursion into the big wide world, we have done all we need. The Ichthus Fellowship who called the march into being have been on the streets since 1974, and I know that the burden of all the organisers of March for Jesus is that the march be used as a launching pad from which Britain can be evangelised continuously during this next decade. They long to see thousands of churches planted in the land. That means that we not only take the idea up at city- or town-wide level, but in our local churches, house groups and also as individuals. If we constantly and prayerfully look for ways and opportunities to allow the Spirit to flow through us wherever we find ourselves, we should begin to make an impact.

Let our teams and national leaders strategise and find ways of working together in the nations; let our local church leaders do the same for our cities, towns and villages; let our house groups think about every street and country lane; and let each individual seek to be a channel for the Spirit wherever they are – at work, at school or at play. Then, and only then, will we ensure that all the dark places of our land are reached. Together, and with the Holy Spirit, we can do this even though it is an awesome task. No one person can do it alone even with the Holy Spirit, and the Holy Spirit himself is limited to working with fallible humanity. From the very beginning God's decision was to work through the church and its members. Through them he will manifest his truth not only on earth but also in heaven. Paul underlines this in Ephesians 3:10 when he declares that '[God's] intent was that now, through the church, the manifold wisdom of God should be made known to the rulers and authorities in the heavenly realms, according to his eternal purpose which he accomplished in Christ Jesus our Lord.'

The Holy Spirit's work in the church in this respect is twofold: to ensure, first, that we are in Christ, and second, that he is in us. Jesus said, 'Remain in me, and I will remain in you…. If you remain in me and my words remain in you, ask whatever you wish, and it will be given you' (Jn 15:4, 7). It's almost as if Jesus struck a kind of bargain with us: 'You want to be in heaven where I am soon to go, and I need more hands and feet on earth where you are staying for the present. So if I abide in you and you abide in me, we'll both get what we need!' We are called to be seated with Christ in heavenly places, while he is looking to work through us here on earth. What a very fair exchange this is and the Holy Spirit is committed to working it out. The more he controls our lives the more effective Christ's ministry in and through us becomes. Ultimately, if our heart beats as one with his heart, we can ask whatever we wish and it shall be done. Here is truly effective living, effective praying and effective evangelism. Why should we go for anything less than God's best?

As we are now seated with Christ on his throne, we are in the place of authority. We can, therefore, manifest the wisdom and authority of God as we deal with the controlling principalities and powers. Because Jesus is the Light of the World, we can be the light of the world. As we humble ourselves before the Lord, God lifts us up and reveals his glory in and through us so that we can say with assurance, 'I no longer live, but Christ lives in me' (Gal 2:20). This may mean that we will be rejected as he was rejected, but at least we shall have the satisfaction of knowing that we are suffering for the right cause and that our lives are making an impact on the powers of darkness. So please, dear Holy Spirit, as we learn to trust in you and to depend on one another, lead us out together to be in the world but not of it, for the glory of Jesus and the salvation of those who are lost. Amen.

12

Into battle 1–demons and evil spirits

Christine

The Holy Spirit wants to work with, in and through us out into the world. He wants to affect our lives to the extent that together with him we move as one, doing the Father's will, glorifying Jesus for all that he has done. What then of other spirits? Demons, fallen angels, principalities, powers, rulers of this world, elemental spirits – where do these beings fit into the scheme of things? Are they real? Can they influence us as individuals or as nations? Is their ambition to move in on our lives, to control and manipulate us into co-operating with the devil? A hierachy among the spiritual forces can be identified in Scripture, among both the heavenly army and the demonic horde. I will examine this in the next chapter but Scripture does not give us much detail. First, we will look at the lowest echelon in Satan's line of command: demons.

The lure of the paranormal

John and I come from vastly different backgrounds. He

was raised in a Christian family – his parents were officers in the Salvation Army. At an young age he came to know the Lord. After the death of his father when he was sixteen years old, John steadily backslid. At the time when we met, he was a hard drinking, smoking and strongly opinionated young man. The first two are long gone; for the third just substitute 'old' for 'young' and you will have a fairly up-to-date picture. The Lord and I are still beavering away in that department!

We met in the era of 'national service'. If you don't understand this term, you're young! At that time all men of eighteen years or over were required to serve two years in some branch of the armed forces. John was in the Irish Guards. There, with little money and not much to do, he began to dabble in the occult, quite successfully. Looking into the past, predicting the future, describing in detail situations, places and scenarios, he soon earned his nickname of 'ghost man'. Regular ouija sessions, with lexicon cards and a glass, were introduced into the barrack room, with some startling effects. John was soon hooked on 'the other side', and the pseudo-supernatural happenings which were becoming more and more a part of his normal experience.

My family were so different from John's. They were religious, but not Christian. Their interest was tea-leaves, fortune-telling, horoscopes, table-rapping, séances and things that go bump in the night. The so called para-normal was very much the normal in our household. It wouldn't have been considered strange if the sitting-room door, which had a faulty catch, swung open, for someone to move over on the settee and say, 'Come on in friend and sit down.' Spirit guides and 'friends' were everyday things to some members of my family, a number of whom have since filtered into the Jehovah's Witnesses or other sects.

We came from the East End of London, historically called the 'sink' of London – the area associated with criminals, graft, poverty, exploitation and human degredation. It was the haunt of Jack the Ripper, a place of gin shops and pawnbrokers. Prostitution – male, female and child – has prospered in this area. And there is deep-rooted superstition. In spite of all this, there is a strong sense of community among the locals and they'll stand together against incredible odds – as was demonstrated during the last war. This solidarity is also true of families who will close ranks against all newcomers. It is a transitory part of London, which has often housed the latest influx of immigrants before they moved on. When I was a child it was a Jewish area, with kosher shops. Now the synagogues have disappeared and mosques have taken their place.

My mother, as I look back, was constantly searching for a supernatural God. She always had me in tow, like a dinghy attached to a larger craft. We dipped into this denomination and that one, always returning to the pseudo-supernatural when we didn't find the real thing in the church. Tragically, she is still searching at nearly eighty years old. She always wants to hear about the amazing things that God can do, but misses Jesus time and time again.

John and I had been giving space in our lives to the enemy left, right and centre. The Bible refers to this as allowing the devil 'room' or 'footholds' (Eph. 4:27 AMPLIFIED). You may wonder: 'How do people become trapped into the occult. What is the occult? How easy is it to become demonised?' Let me share one personal experience and then come back to some of these questions.

John and I finally came to the Lord through all this mess of occult involvement. In discovering the reality of evil spirits we were forced to consider the fact that Jesus has power over them and in the end we yielded to him.

One of our first dates was a séance, where we experienced automatic writing, manifestations and flying objects. We used the ouija board on our own after we were married, and something happened in this setting which was a very real turning-point for us. The glass asked us to repeat

the Lord's Prayer backwards. This request made me feel a
bit uncomfortable, but for John, with his Christian upbringing, it was a definite 'No'. We began to read the Bible
and try out different churches. With my family
background, it was simply history repeating itself. But just
before Christmas 1959, at a carol service in a Baptist
church, John turned around and the Lord healed his
backsliding. It had nothing to do with the service or Christmas. Jesus revealed himself and John came out a different
man. I, however, was just the same! Now I understand that
we were both in a process and several months later, I
decided to 'give the Lord Jesus a whirl', and we have been
whirling around together ever since then, for almost thirty-
two years.

With all this demonic activity in John's past and mine,
the crunch eventually had to come. One evening we were
sitting in the living-room, on either side of the fire. By now
we had both been filled with the Spirit, in the same place
but not at the same time. We were baptised in water and in
the Spirit at a mission in Three Colts Lane, Bethnal Green,
London, close to where Booth started the Salvation Army
– a significant fact for John and for me it was close to my
old home in the East End. The Lord often seems to use our
roots and history to complete things for us; he truly is
amazing. This particular evening the children were tucked
up in bed; all was quiet and relaxed. Suddenly, I was aware
of a feeling of constriction in my chest and in my throat.
John and I were alone in the room together and it seemed
as though an unseen pair of hands was gradually squeezing
the life out of me. I remember being extremely afraid and
thinking that I was about to die. I looked across at John
and saw that his eyes were wide and that there was a look
of horror on his face. When we exchanged experiences
later, he told me that he actually thought he was losing his
mind.

As our eyes met we recognised that something supernaturally evil was happening to us both at the same time. With difficulty we stood up, held hands, almost supporting one another, and began to praise God with our new Holy Spirit tongues language. As we gained courage and strength so we experienced something physically leaving us. Even today, the experience is still so real to us that we can remember through which corner of the room the dark shapeless mass left. Afterwards, we walked round the house, visiting each room and praying over the kids that the Holy Spirit would inhabit our home in a new way.

Satan's footholds

How easy is it to become demonised? Can a Christian have a demon? It is my belief and experience that most people are influenced by demons and that Christians are no exception. Just a word of explanation here. I would never use the word 'possessed' in this connection myself. The only spirit which can truly possess, own, take over and be fused with my spirit – to the point where it is difficult to see where one finishes and another begins – is the Holy Spirit. This is why New Testament translators are in some confusion at times as to whether the Bible refers to the human spirit or to the Holy Spirit. The Greek word *daimonizomai* is better translated 'to be demonised', or vexed by, or troubled by a demon, than 'possessed', which comes from the understanding current in the period when the Scriptures were first translated into English and does not properly convey the biblical meaning.

We can, however, give Satan and his minions footholds in our lives, and they will always take whatever they can get. The Holy Spirit, on the other hand, takes only what we freely give. He never goes beyond, or encroaches on fresh ground that hasn't been offered to him. Demons seize any opportunity, taking more and more, insidiously, until there is an area in our lives where we effectively are not in control. The Bible deals very clearly with foot-holds. We are instructed in Ephesians 4:27 to make sure that we do not give our Enemy any ground. In Matthew 16:23 Jesus rounds on Peter saying, 'Out of my sight, Satan!' This incident shows us that Peter's very love for the Lord, and his rejection of the thought of his Master's death, motivated him out of sentiment rather than obedience to God's plan. Satan himself used this toehold to manipulate Peter.

As you've read what I've said about the way demons influence people, I trust that you have come to understand how they can manipulate Christians. John and I were positively delivered from demonic forces after we became Christians and were filled with the Holy Spirit. No demon can be fused with the spirit of a man or woman who is born of God, but they can manoeuvre and exploit us through our weaknesses and the footholds in our lives. It is all a matter of degree; the more we yield ourselves to temptation, the greater the Enemy's power over us. We have no need to fear provided we are open to the correction and discipline of the Spirit. Peter tells us that the goal of our faith is the salvation of our souls (1 Pet 1:9). 'Born of the Spirit' is where we begin; we must work through the areas of weakness in our minds, wills and emotions until our souls are totally redeemed – that's where we're heading.

Footholds are not only areas of occult involvement but any point of weakness in our lives or character. The Enemy latches on to these and uses them to control our actions. If we have succumbed to the Enemy's temptations and, for example, are awash in over-sentimentality or habitually tell lies, or do any one of a thousand other things which give him space, we need to repent and, with the Holy Spirit's help, turn from the sin. Thus the Enemy loses his grip and is driven from us. The letter to the Ephesians also highlights some of these foothold areas, such as lying, anger, stealing, laziness, bad language, gossip, bitterness, slander and malice. All these are ground in which evil spirits can take root and grow strong.

Deliverance from demons

Their power has to be broken and sometimes deliverance is needed. This usually comes with the help of those gifted and experienced in this field. The compulsion the demon has brought into our lives is ended and we are free to choose to do the will of God. Now begins the process period when, through temptation and trial, we walk in our new-found liberty. The initial battle is won but the war is not yet over. Now we have to resist temptation in the power of the Holy Spirit from that place of freedom. James 4:7 gives us a double-edged weapon which, if we use it, assures us of continued victory: 'Submit yourselves, then, to God. Resist the devil, and he will flee from you.' The New Testament makes it plain that Jesus recognised, was acknowledged by and dealt with demons. This was not, however, his whole ministry, only a part.

Not every sin, sickness or misdemeanour was dealt with as being directly demonic. In Luke 8:48 the woman who had an issue of blood was told that her faith had made her whole. There is no reference here to demons, but verses 29 to 32 record that Jesus had commanded the evil spirit to leave a tortured demoniac, and not just one but a whole host of demons fled from the man. We too must take care to make these distinctions as we lean heavily on the Holy Spirit and his gifts. When does a person need to be healed, when delivered, when rebuked or admonished? Only the Holy Spirit can help us to differentiate and bestow upon us his gifts to deal with such a variety of causes.

Matthew 12:24–29 begins to hint at the organisation of our Enemy's kingdom, which is vastly different to God's, for here Beelzebub reigns. Jesus states clearly that he himself drives out demons by the power of the Spirit of God.

Hallelujah, that same Spirit is available to us today. In Mark 1:23-27 we see that demons can speak through men's mouths. They recognise Jesus, calling him the 'Holy One of God' and clearly acknowledge his right to deal with them. Demons are looking for human hosts to devour and to manipulate into destroying one another. They use us to vilify, to separate and even kill one another. They seek to use us like puppets. The Holy Spirit is looking for men and women to be his hands, his feet, his voice, his heart in this sin-wrecked world. He demonstrates his power over Satan by cutting the puppets' strings.

Demons know who God, Jesus and the Holy Spirit are. In James 2:19 we are told that they believe and shudder before God. That's a terrific picture to hold in our minds – not a strong Enemy but a shuddering jelly. Wonderful! They have, however, been allowed considerable powers and are sometimes involved in causing mental disorder, sickness, dumbness, and can control humans and animals. Instances of all these can be found in the Gospels. In every case Jesus dislodged and disarmed the demon, setting the prisoner free. Let us join the fight and get on the victorious side with the Lord Jesus. Let us be his disciples, following in his footsteps, equipped with the same Holy Spirit. Let us be doers and not simply hearers of the word, and together wage war on the demonic forces in the lives of men and women.

Of course, we must do this with care and sensitivity and also in consultation with others in our church. One reason many avoid this area of Christian warfare is because often those who do venture to get involved, work in isolation and end up with all kinds of strange practices and beliefs. For example, I have heard it said on the basis of Hebrews 4:12 'the word of God...penetrates even to dividing spirit and soul, joints and marrow...' that demons get lodged and live in the tiny gaps between bone and marrow! And I have been reprimanded for refusing to send demons 'back to the pit from whence they came'. My critics were rightly concerned that the evil spirit would wander looking for another home, but they forget that that is exactly what Jesus said would happen. He pointed out that if we only clean out the room, but do not fill it, the spirit will return with seven others (Mt 12:43–45). Again in Matthew 8:29 and Luke 4:34 the demons made it clear that they knew there was a time appointed for their destruction. Jesus could have ordered demons into the abyss and cleared the whole world out for that matter, but they still have their part to play in bringing forth the harvest of good and evil so that they can be safely reaped to everlasting life or destruction. We must take care that in our fervour we do not try to accomplish more than Jesus.

Our bad habits can become the breeding-ground for bondage to Satan. Smoking is a good example. How often I have heard the words 'I can give it up any time I want.' All too frequently this is simply not true. A man I know tried everything to stop smoking. He went to a therapist for help, but there was no way he could stop. His doctor prescribed a special chewing-gum. All was well while he chewed the gum, but when he attempted to stop chewing, he started smoking once again. He was addicted to nicotine. He was prayed for and by the power of the Holy Spirit the compulsion was dealt with and he was set free. At present, although tempted to smoke from time to time, he hasn't gone back one step, praise God! Crisis and process are equally necessary ingredients in our lives.

I was approached by a young woman who had a history of miscarriage. She and her husband were desperate to have a baby and asked me to pray for her. As we prayed, the Holy Spirit revealed through a word of knowledge that her family was involved in Freemasonry. She agreed that this was true, and after some discussion on the subject she saw that she, personally, had to repudiate this. She also saw that she needed God's forgiveness for her wrong attitude to this 'religion' in her life. The power was broken, the spirit ejected, and I'm thrilled to say that many months on she has produced a lovely baby. It is a fact that we are affected by the historic involvements of our families. The Old Testament warns that the sins of the fathers are visited upon the children; in the same way we may receive many blessings through a godly heritage. Although we know that in Christ we are forgiven and our historic accounts are cleared, nevertheless often a residue of effects needs to be dealt with. We may not always understand all the nuances of this but experience proves it. Recently, I heard back from a lady who suffered from anorexia some time ago. When I originally prayed for her the Holy Spirit revealed to me that her problem was low self-esteem, not the anorexia at all – that was just a by-product. To try to explain, the anorexia was like huge flowers on a bush; you might cut the flowers over and over again, but they would continue to bloom. To destroy the flowers, the plant must be dug up at the root. The demon of low self-esteem was dealt with that day, and so far her preoccupation with weight-loss and starvation has gone; she's free! Not everyone with anorexia or bulimia has a spirit of low self-esteem. In my experience, the same symptoms or compulsions do not necessarily have the same root cause. As always, we rely on the Holy Spirit, not on what has happened before in similar circumstances.

I once prayed for a man who had a bad back. I didn't sense that he was demonised but I was aware that there was a foothold somewhere in his past. Again, the Lord uncovered the territory through a word of knowledge. The man had failed to forgive someone for an incident in the past which caused bitterness. He spoke out the words of forgiveness and received forgiveness for his own hardness of heart. You could hear the bones crack back into place as the Lord healed him.

Often Christians are fascinated with demons and the 'dark side', and we must take care not to become preoccupied or taken up with them in a wrong way, lest we glorify our Enemy. We want neither to see demons under every piece of furniture or round every corner, nor to be ostriches burying our heads in the sand and denying or ignoring their existence and powers.

There are, of course, other ways of controlling the demonic forces which seek to run amok through individuals in our localities. Roger Forster, leader of the Ichthus Christian Fellowship, tells of a number of occasions when the group has taken up press reports of murder and robbery and prayed for God's intervention, with startling results. At one time they were counselling a man whose father had been killed by a murderer who was on the loose. The murderer continually terrorised one of the areas where the fellowship met. Twelve hundred people gathered at their monthly celebration meeting and five separate messages arrived on the platform mentioning the notorious criminal. So every one of the 1,200 people went to prayer. 'Lord, no more murders please. Apprehend the criminal quickly and alert the Christian police to follow-ups, letters and tip-offs.' There were no further incidents and within thirty-six hours the police had caught the culprit. After telling this story at Spring Harvest, Roger found a man waiting for him as he stepped down from the platform. The man revealed that his father, a Christian policeman, had followed up a most unlikely tip-off which led to the arrest and conviction of the killer.

The occult

Let's take a brief look at the word 'occult'. The dictionary definition is 'kept secret, mysterious, beyond the range of ordinary knowledge, conceal, cut off from view by passing in front of'. All these phrases reveal something to us but the last definition paints a very clear picture of how involvement in any way with the occult comes between, and cuts us off, from God.

Occult practice in the Bible is seen in the form of mediums, who are spiritists claiming to traffic with the dead (Lev 19:31). Also mentioned is divination, foretelling and interpreting dreams. The Egyptians were heavily into this, and Moses commanded that those who participated in such things be stoned (Deut 18:9–13). Necromancy, worshipping the dead and consulting the dead appear in the same passage and are described as detestable in the Lord's sight. Soothsaying, casting spells and astrology are condemned not only in the Old Testament, but in Acts 16:16 are clearly recognised as demon activity to be driven out. In Isaiah 2:6 soothsayers and diviners are referred to as superstitions from the East. Nothing new comes from Satan. He is not a creative being; he rehashes all his old ways, giving them a new coat of glitter, thus hoping to ensnare a fresh generation. Sorcery, magic spells, witchcraft, spiritism and all who practise them are condemned unless they repent and turn to Christ.

There is what might be termed a soft side to the occult. Palm-reading, fortune-telling and tea-leaves are often acceptable at a church fête. Astrology, cartomancy and ouija boards are all projected to be a 'bit of harmless fun'. I think of the dangers of the occult in picture form. I see the shape of a funnel. Funnels are wonderful things. If you put something in it will inevitably be drawn down to the tiny narrow open-ended point. Be seduced by the so-called soft side, which is at the wide end, and you may find yourself inside a slippery funnel, going deep down into darkness. Once in, there will be plenty to give you just enough encouragement to continue the downward motion.

So you've been told you are somewhat psychic and that this is a gift which needs developing. I fell for that one. There's no way you're in touch with dead loved ones, but with demons.

Here's another picture for you. This is of a school for

demons. You could call it 'The Demonic School of Imper-
sonation'. In the classes they practise imitating people's
voices and mannerisms, just like a TV impressionist. At
the right moment they step forward, enter the medium, do
their act and you are convinced it was Mum, Dad, Julie,
Tom or some other loved one. It's so easy to be deceived.

Spiritism, precognition, astral travel, clairvoyants, tele-
pathy, trances, automatic writing, ghosts, poltergeists,
witches' covens, satanists, Masons – the list of occult
activities goes on and on. The sides of the funnel may well
be lined with friends and family who are themselves trapped, and you may need deliverance before you are truly
free. An excellent book on the whole subject, in greater
detail than I can give here, is *Paganism and the Occult* by
Kevin Logan (Kingsway). But with all this, never forget
that our enemy uses very ordinary things to ensnare unsus-
pecting victims. Perhaps materialism itself may be the
major bait he will use, as Scripture warns that 'the love of
money is a root of all kinds of evil' (2 Tim 6:10).

The New Age movement

Nevertheless, there is one other area of concern which I
must touch on before concluding this chapter – the New
Age movement. A great deal has been written and said
about New Age, so it shouldn't be difficult to find some lit-
erature if you wish to be informed, but take care as there's
also a lot of rubbish and speculation about. On the positive
side, a number of genuine concerns are expressed through
New Age teaching, including care for the environment,
women's rights and the reassertion of spiritual values over
material. Christians would do well to examine these issues
and determine what our response should be. If we remain
uninformed and have no contribution to make we will have
failed our generation.

However, behind the façade of what appears to be good

lies a hotch-potch of all the old evils, grouped together with the desire to bring about a new world order and government. Of course, the inspiration behind this kind of thinking is Lucifer, who adorns himself as an angel of light but is intent on deceiving and captivating the souls of men. To this end he introduces many subtle counterfeits which either delude by leading genuine seekers astray, or hinder those who see through them from finding the reality of what the Holy Spirit is saying about important worldwide concerns. This is a tragedy as thousands of Christians are paralysed with fear, viewing the whole of this present charismatic movement and many of the secular social movements as being of the devil, or at least something to be regarded with suspicion.

The message, therefore, to those of us who enjoy the blessing of Pentecost, is threefold: watch carefully to block infiltration of wrong New Age ideas and methods; be sensitive towards those who have been damaged by being deceived or turned off by these teachings and practices; claim back the ground which Lucifer has taken.

Let me pick up the last point and illustrate what I mean. Some years ago, John started the Rainbow Company, which is now part of the Servant Group. We were at Greenbelt, selling T-shirts and novelties, many of which had rainbows in the design. John was approached by a well known international author who was wandering round the tent with a frown on his face. 'Do you realise what the rainbow symbolises?' he asked. 'Yes,' was the instant reply, 'it is a sign of God's promise to mankind.' 'Ah, but didn't you know the New Agers have adopted it as their logo?' 'Yes,' said John again, 'but I have claimed it back for the Lord!'

You may feel that the story is trite, but I don't think so. The Enemy steals our ground little by little, till in the end we retreat into a totally defensive mode. Because New Age cares for the earth, is pioneering for women's rights, is into wholistic medicine and healing and is concerned for unity, we dare not vacate these areas and passively surrender them. We must find the Holy Spirit's answer and take this territory for Jesus. It will not be gained without a battle, but we have the promise that every place where the soles of our feet tread shall be ours.

Let's start with the phrase 'New Age' itself, which actually belongs to our God and has been hijacked. We are looking for the new age which John foresaw in Revelation 21, 'a new heaven and a new earth, for the first heaven and the first earth had passed away'.

The devil's decade of vengeance

When we look to the heart of what is happening through New Age – the occult and witchcraft – we find a fearsome unity of evil emerging, not imaginary but real. As the church almost unanimously embarks on a decade of evangelism to take us into the year 2,000, so Satan's forces are banding together. The thought that Satans's 'church' also has denominations seems incredible, but it is true. These 'demonic denominations' historically have been at loggerheads, the satanists feeling they have the purest form of their religion and refusing to associate with the Wiccan circle and other groups whose theology is suspect. Among this unholy band, however, unity is emerging. They have declared a decade of vengeance, to coincide with the church's evangelistic thrust.

In piecing together the diabolical plan, Christians are beginning to hear from members of the various factions who have turned to Christ of a considerable increase in the most vile practice of all – human sacrifice. Women, it seems, are deliberately becoming pregnant, receiving no antenatal care, and when the child is born the birth is not registered with the authorities. In this way, ready-made human sacrifices are available, unnamed, unrecorded and therefore there is no hue and cry at the disappearance of a child. The scheme is truly sickening. We read in our newspapers of unmarked graves and bones being unearthed. Often blame is placed on child pornography rings, but perhaps we are being shielded from the truth, particularly when the truth might be too horrendous for us to come to terms with. Only a united Holy Spirit-baptised church led by Jesus can hope to stand against such wickedness.

One thing is sure, as 2 Peter 2:4–10 declares:

> For if God did not spare angels when they sinned, but sent them to hell, putting them into gloomy dungeons to be held for judgment; if he did not spare the ancient world when he brought the flood on its ungodly people, but protected Noah, a preacher of righteousness, and seven others; if he condemned the cities of Sodom and Gomorrah by burning them to ashes, and made them an example of what is going to happen to the ungodly; and if he rescued Lot, a righteous man, who was distressed by the filthy lives of lawless men...if this is so, then the Lord knows how to rescue godly men from trials and to hold the unrighteous for the day of judgment, while continuing their punishment. This is especially true of those who follow the corrupt desire of the sinful nature and despise authority.

God will indeed judge and destroy the wicked and protect the righteous; we can trust him totally.

13

Into battle 2 – principalities and powers

Christine

And there was war in heaven. Michael and his angels fought against the dragon, and the dragon and his angels fought back. But he was not strong enough, and they lost their place in heaven. The great dragon was hurled down – that ancient serpent called the devil or Satan, who leads the whole world astray. He was hurled to the earth, and his angels with him (Rev 12:7–9).

For our struggle is not against flesh and blood, but against the rulers, against the authorities, against the powers of this dark world and against the spiritual forces of evil in the heavenly realms (Eph 6:12).

What pictures these scriptures conjure up in the mind – Satan, desiring the kingdom of God for his own. Did he become so demented that he could think for one minute that he might win? He fought Michael and his angels but he just wasn't strong enough. There's a phrase to remember when you are hard up against it and under attack: he wasn't strong enough! He lost the fight and was hurled down to earth where he leads the whole world astray. So our battle is not against flesh and blood – mere human beings – but something behind them, the grinning skull which only shows through from time to time.

Who's who – spiritual beings

What can we learn from Scripture about the spiritual hierarchy? First and foremost, leading the evil host in this spiritual battle, is Satan. In the passage from Revelation 12 we have a descriptive word picture of what Satan is like: 'great dragon', 'ancient serpent', 'devil or Satan', and later, 'accuser of the brethren'. He is the commander-in-chief as he was in that original rebellion. To this very day he continues manipulating people and deploying his troops. He is the father of lies. He does not have the godly attributes of omniscience, omnipotence and omnipresence. He is a created being, along with all others, apart from God himself. It's a great comfort to know that he can't be everywhere at once, or know our every thought; that is the prerogative of God alone. Satan is mighty and deceptive but he is defeated, resistible and limited; he is not by any means all powerful.

The second line of command in this hellish army are the 'fallen angels'. Revelation 12:4 gives us to understand that when Satan lost his battle to usurp the throne of God, one third of the angels were thrown down with him. When it comes to the realm of angelic beings, the Scriptures give little information. There are no clear job descriptions or lines of command. We can read, here and there, of angels, archangels, seraphim, cherubim, guardians, and so on. Some try to chart the host of heaven, but they appear to me to be stretching Scripture. It would have been simple for the Lord to give us such information if it were necessary.

Over and over again in the Gospels we see Jesus swatting demons like flies. He deals with them in cases of dumbness, fortune-telling, sickness and madness with speed and ease. We are not clearly told how they came to be in their present sphere of influence, so I take it that we don't need to know. What we *can* be sure of is our authority, under Jesus, over these spirits.

There is, however, an amazing amount of information about angels. Billy Graham in his book *Angels*, says that there are 300 mentions in Scripture, and these disclose that God has countless numbers ready to obey his commands. They also reveal that some are reserved to aid us in our struggle against Satan and his corps. Gaining more insight into the purpose and ministry of angels helps us to understand the strengths and weaknesses of our enemies, the fallen angels. For example, 2 Samuel 14:20 explains that angels possess knowledge. They understand what is happening and are wise, but Mark 13:32 makes it quite clear that they don't know everything. So although they are intelligent, thinking, reasoning beings, they don't comprehend the whole of God's plan. Fallen angels, once removed from God's presence and maimed, as they are by their rebellion, are usually in the dark as to God's real purpose and objectives in the lives of his saints.

This is starkly illustrated in the story of Job. Satan imagined that he was really going to grind Job to a powder. He just could not understand or perceive that God was merely using him to bring Job into a closer relationship with himself.

Angels are also supernaturally strong; it took only one to kill all the firstborn in Egypt, and only one to close the lions' mouths for Daniel. Nowhere in Scripture are we given to understand that the fallen angels and Lucifer were totally denuded of their power. What we are told in Colossians 2:15 is that Jesus, 'having disarmed the powers and authorities...made a public spectacle of them, triumphing over them by the cross', not by making them powerless but by the greater power of his perfect sacrificial obedience! Thus he opened the way for us to overcome the present and limited powers of evil through that same cross. Otherwise fallen angels would not be around today to continue their vile work. 1 John 4:4 underlines this and gives us comfort: 'Greater is he that is in you than he that is in the world' (AV).

Now, perhaps, the lines of authority are becoming clearer to us than before. The devil stands alone in evil and authority. Some people argue that he was once an archangel along with Michael, equal to, or even his superior. Isaiah 14:4 and the following verses talk about Babylon, but verse 12 changes, identifying the power behind the Babylonian throne as Lucifer. There are five statements of Satan's will in verses 13 and 14, uncovering his plan to replace God as ruler of heaven and earth, in fact of the whole universe. Below the devil are the fallen angels who obey his commands, carrying out his orders and plans. Knowing, as we do, that he cannot be everywhere at once, he has to delegate. In Daniel 10:13 we read of the battle between the 'messenger from God' and the 'prince of Persia', two angelic beings fighting it out in the heavens. The messenger angel may well have been Gabriel, whom God often used in this capacity. It was certainly Gabriel who spoke to Daniel on two other occasions. It was also Gabriel who visited Zechariah, telling him that he would remain dumb until his son's birth, and Mary at Nazareth to announce to her God's favour and the coming upon her of the Holy Spirit that Jesus might be born.

Back in Daniel we see, in the prince of Persia, a fallen angel of similar rank and power. God's messenger angel needed help from Michael, the prince of Israel himself, in order to break away to visit Daniel. Elsewhere, there is mention of the king of Persia resisting God's messenger – is this, once again, the grinning skull showing through? Behind Cyrus, the king of Persia, is there a heavenly evil to be reckoned with? I believe so. Isn't this a clear example of a man, albeit a king, being used and manipulated by the Enemy for his own ends.

Colossians 1:16 speaks about 'all things...created...visible and invisible, whether thrones or powers or rulers or authorities'. Here, as in other scriptures, there is a definite link between the seen and the unseen, heavenly powers and earthly rulers.

We see this same power behind the throne, in Ezekiel 28. This prophecy is against the king of Tyre, a human king, but in verse 13 we hear that he was 'in Eden, the garden of God'. It is not possible that the king of Tyre was present when sin first entered the human arena all those centuries before; Lucifer was there in the garden, no doubt with some of his fiendish friends. At that time man had not multiplied over the earth and so these evil beings didn't have a great deal to do. My guess is that a crowd were in on that first temptation, laughing and enjoying the thought of the pain they would cause God and man through separation. So here again we see a force beyond Cyrus – the king of Tyre – making us aware that we don't fight flesh and blood but evil principalities and powers in high places.

What was true in Bible times remains true today, and God would have us recognise the satanic powers behind many of our worldly institutions and structures. Unless we do this our success in warfare will be limited, for we must engage and bind the Enemy in the heavens and also in practical ways on earth. Traditionally, charismatics have had half a truth and evangelical social activists the other half as the one group has stormed the heavens and the other has battled on earth. These two must come together to wage a common warfare otherwise Satan will remain the power behind the earthly thrones.

Countering Satan

The love of money is the root of all evil. In Matthew 6:24 Jesus spells it out for us. We cannot serve two masters; we cannot serve God and money. The currency of the kingdom of the world is gold; the currency of the kingdom of God is service.

The kingdoms of this world and their wealth were Satan's to offer Jesus in the wilderness and he rejected them out of hand. That power and wealth are still, for the present, in the devil's hand, and he offers them as incentives to anyone who will bow down and serve his purpose today. Satan remains behind the scenes controlling the massive wealth which is in the hands of so few.

As servants of the Master our commission is clearly laid out for us. Isaiah 58 underlines to us where our energies should be channelled. We must be concerned with injustice, oppression, food, shelter and clothing. Our interests must lie in the direction of our 'own flesh and blood' (v 7). Isaiah is not speaking just of family here, encouraging us to look after the interests and welfare of our own kin. Jesus himself posed the question as to who were his mother and father, brothers and sisters. This is not said to diminish or ignore our family ties, more to challenge and enlarge our understanding of God's love for all people. The flesh and blood referred to in Isaiah 58 is suffering humanity itself. Jesus died for all – past, present and future – and we must labour to bring them the good news until he comes again.

Luke 4:21 tells us Jesus read from the Book of Isaiah and declared that the prophecies were fulfilled in him that very day. Here again we see the role of the Holy Spirit emphasised, 'The Spirit of the Lord is on me...' (Lk 4:18). Filled with the Holy Spirit, Jesus could move forward into his ministry. The Holy Spirit, together with the angels who were Jesus' constant companions, was the power behind the Man. The Spirit and the angels are also the spiritual powers behind the church. We are, therefore, equipped to meet Satan and his supporters on their terms, in the heavens and in earthly authorities. All power was given to Jesus from the throne of God, and it is on that basis that he tells us to go and make disciples of all nations.

We must be engaged in spiritual warfare at all levels. So often we settle for forays into the personal, individual demon level and we become euphoric at the occasional healings and deliverances we see. OK, but don't let's stay there, good as it may be. Let us train our guns on new targets as we search out the powers who move in wider spheres. Let's look behind the evil systems, structures and ideologies of this world, and enter the arena of intercession, words, persuasion, laws, governments, councils, wealth and human endeavour, always and only in the power of the Holy Spirit. Let us see the angels – those who oppose and those who support us – as real supernatural beings, not as cottonwool or candy-floss fairies, flitting daintily around with long wings and see-through bodies. There's a real war on; there may be casualties and we must be prepared to fight in both the heavenly and the earthly realms. May God keep us from being so heavenly minded that we are no earthly good, or so earth-bound that we fail to see ourselves rightfully seated in heavenly places.

Systems which reduce people to grinding poverty, taking away their human rights; structures which are concerned with amassing and keeping wealth in order to gain more and more power; greed which robs and rapes the earth of its resources, polluting sea and air; ideologies and religions which have 'a form of godliness but deny the power', are all to be challenged and torn down to make way for the King of kings and Lord of lords. Our individuality and personal freedom must not stand in the way of our working together in the church. Those things which make Christians enemies must also be dealt with. Slander, mistrust, past hurts, rejections, misunderstandings and bad communication have to go so that we become the visible army of God. The church's calling is to identify, uncover and deal with these powers. When we stand together, with a God-given common purpose, the Spirit will fall on us. That first visitation of the Holy Spirit on the Day of Pentecost was a corporate experience (as were many that followed), and that kind of baptism must take place again. How much more powerful is the outcome when not just one man, or one woman, empowered by the Holy Spirit, is speaking in tongues and preaching in the marketplace, but 120 of them; not just one or two languages but many. Initially the crowd was confused, but 3,000 were swept into the kingdom on that day. This kind of church, moving together in the baptism of the Holy Spirit and fire, is a sign, a red rag to the bull, daring our enemy to charge if he will.

As we start to challenge the authorities we may need to fast and pray to discover what we are up against in a given geographical area. Some historical research may help to uncover or throw light on the Enemy's plans. Frequently, the natural and spiritual go hand in hand. This applies to localities as well as to nations. Those of us who live in the West are in some ways still trading off our history of Christianity, but, just like the prodigal, we are squandering our inheritance. Other nations are even now reaping the harvest of having publicly burned their Bibles, rejecting God or even declaring him to be dead. These things have repercussions in a spiritual realm as well as in the earthly sphere as the two are interlocked. One affects the other, both from God's and Satan's perspective.

Perhaps you find that people do not exactly reject the gospel in your area but are just plain not interested. You might do well to explore your local history a little; the Lord may open your eyes to another dimension of warfare. When you have more understanding you may discover the grinning skull, that specific principality who rules over your particular town or county. Then is the moment to do battle in the two realms by pushing back the darkness on earth and joining in the fight which rages in the heavenlies. Remember Jesus' words as he gave his disciples the keys: 'Whatever you bind on earth will be bound in heaven, and whatever you loose on earth will be loosed in heaven' (Mt

16:19; 18:18). And one legitimate contemporary rendering of those amazing words could be, 'Whatever you forbid, will be forbidden, whatever you permit, will be permitted.'

In this respect, I know of one group who were suffering from quite serious oppression from their local council. Rather than being defeated by the opposition, they turned to prayer and spiritual warfare when their efforts at ground level failed. Certain councillors, who were extremely resistant and openly antagonistic, were remarkably removed from office. Following the council's refusal to publicise the group's part in a major local festival because of their stance on Christian ethics, local residents joined the debate. They insisted that the church's musicians actually led the festival parade, and thus the council had to relent and supply free printed advertising for all three evangelistic meetings which were to be held during the event.

There are countless examples of this kind of remarkable change in circumstances from areas of the world where the church is restricted by unsympathetic governments. We should expect to see more and more of the Spirit's intervention in society as we take advantage of our Enemy's efforts to squash the work of God.

On a quite different tack, but still on the subject of the church invading territory controlled by evil principalities and powers, Dr Patrick Dixon's story is worthy of mention. The AIDS tragedy was just about to hit the UK. Patrick Dixon had simple ambitions to lead the Ealing Christian Fellowship, of which he was a part, and any thoughts of being involved in a national initiative were a million miles from his thinking. He had gone to one of Gerald Coates' pioneer leaders conferences hoping for some direction from the Lord, but none came. At the end of the weekend Gerald found him looking somewhat dejected. 'Patrick,' he said, 'you will never lead ECF. Your gifts will be used in an altogether different area which has something to do with your medical background.' On his way home Gerald considered what he had said. 'I must be mad,' he thought. 'Penicillin has been invented!'

Later, Dr Dixon's work in terminal care brought him into contact with AIDS victims. Something had to be done. His response was to write *The Truth About AIDS* for Kingsway Publications. A grant-making trust heard about the book and the counselling work which had begun in a small way. It donated £500,000 to what is now ACET (AIDS Care, Education and Training) which today cares for more dying AIDS patients in their own homes than any other independent charity in the UK. They also run the largest training programme in schools and colleges in the country. A timely supernatural word from God changed the whole course of one man's life, and now thousands around the nation are reaping the benefit.

The Spirit's cleansing

Let me finish this chapter by relating two visions. The first relates to the realm of individual demons, which I trust will aid you in sharpening your spiritual weapons. The second is concerned with our corporate response to spiritual powers, and I pray will challenge you to commit yourself to the church as a whole.

The first vision I had some time ago and it has really helped me in my fight against demons and the power they retain in so many people's lives. The Lord showed me a bath, in a field. Like my husband, you may have great difficulty with some of my pictures. When I started to tell him this one, he asked, 'What is a bath doing in a field?' This bath was full of rubbish and had a shower over it. The shower was on, but just a little dribble of water was coming through, so there was some water in the bath discoloured by all the junk. I began to remove, layer by layer, what was in the bath. Finally, I had a pile on the floor beside me, my sleeves were rolled up to my armpits and I was thrusting my arms through the dirty water. Then the Lord asked me a question: 'Why is the bath not empty Christine?' By now I was, to say the least, just a touch frustrated. 'If I knew, Lord, why it wasn't empty, I would do something about it!' was my rather curt reply. The Lord is infinitely patient with us and understanding. Very lovingly he said, 'Think about it.' I did and suddenly it was as if a light went on in my head. 'The plug is in,' I almost shouted. 'Yes,' said Father. 'What would have happened if you had just pulled out the plug at the beginning and turned the shower on full?' Things really began to fall into place. It seems that the Lord was teaching me a principle. 'Everything would have been washed down the drain,' I said. 'Exactly,' said the Lord. Find the stopper and let the Holy Spirit do the work.

The trend, in the area of deliverance, seems to be to supply people with a manual. Certain behaviour patterns can be interpreted into a demonic family tree. You follow the lines back carefully through the structure, arrive at a certain demon and cast that out, plus six to two dozen others along the route. If it really is that simple, why doesn't the New Testament give us these family trees and why didn't Jesus, who is our Example, use this type of device, and what part does the gift of discernment play if you can rely on a detailed and identifiable plan? My vision of the bath seemed to clarify some issues for me. The bath was the person's life, the rubbish, accumulated Enemy dumping, the shower was God's Spirit. Cleaning out the garbage which has been pitched in takes time, months or even years. Finally, you still have the dirty water.

The answer, I saw, was to ask the Holy Spirit to reveal at the very beginning what the plug was. A plug is such a small thing to hold in so much water. Jesus always knew what the plug was. He didn't go in for multiple or protracted deliverances. A command and a name and the demon was gone even where there was a legion! The disciples too were obviously really blessed when they functioned in the same way.

Discovering the plug will come through words of knowledge or discernment, and the deliverance should leave the person unscathed. The Lord was always concerned for the human dignity of the person he was helping. He rarely allowed demons to roll people around on the floor or behave in an unseemly fashion for very long before dealing with them. The only words or sounds he allowed to come from them acknowledged him as Lord, the Son of the living God. I personally would be delighted for us to be dealing with demons who call out our names and identify us as sons and daughters of the living God. Sadly, this doesn't often seem to be the case. I know my name is written down in heaven but, like Paul, I also have an ambition to be recognised as God's ambassador in hell.

It is not enough to pull the plug; we must switch the shower on. To put it another way, Jesus taught that having swept out the room, we are to fill it. Simply casting the demon out will not guarantee permanent freedom, for if the life is not occupied by the Holy Spirit, then the demon will return, bringing others with him. The second state is then worse than the first.

The doomed castle

In my second vision I was on a beach and saw in the distance a hugh castle with battlements, moat and drawbridge. As I approached the castle it became larger and larger, until it loomed over me, blotting out the sun and bringing a sense of doom, darkness and despair. I stood there, with my head thrown back, looking up at the towering sides. It looked utterly indestructible and fearsome and I was terrified. I turned to run and its shadow seemed to fall everywhere. I saw the sea quite far out, but just on the turn. I heard the Lord say, 'Be part of the ocean Christine,' and suddenly I was running into the sea and found myself becoming part of it. Now I was in the turning tide.

The water crept slowly up the beach, higher and higher, nearer and nearer to the terrible fortifications. A wave fell gently on to the side of the castle. What was happening? I couldn't quite see. Another wave lapped around the far side of the castle. Nothing could stop the tide from coming in. Waves were now breaking over the walls I could see something was happening. The castle was breaking down – it was actually crumbling away. A larger wave than before ran up the beach and the wall was breached; a gaping hole appeared in the side. The tide advanced and more waves broke over the doomed fortress – why, the whole thing was made from sand! No part of the structure could withstand the sea. The waves crashed right over what remained and when they fell back, there was no trace of the castle left at all – not a wall, not a stone, not even a dent or vestige. It had all been utterly washed away, leaving a perfectly smooth beach behind.

What a picture of Satan's downfall! His power has already been broken by our Lord Jesus in the heavens, and that means his earthly structures cannot endure. It is now the task of the church, the corporate body of Christ, to expose and oppose every earthly satanic stronghold, at the same time revealing Jesus as the only means of salvation. Having overcome the world in the power of the Holy Spirit, we will lay our trophy at Jesus' feet. But his promise is to place it firmly in our hands, for he declared that the meek would inherit the earth. Those who are faithful in battle now are destined to rule and reign with him in the future.

14

Witnesses to the end!

John

I've heard many stories about Christians 'witnessing' but two stand out in my mind above the rest. The first took place in a sleepy Cornish village. A group of saints had retreated to a small Christian guest-house for their holiday. One morning, as they were going through their spiritual exercises before being forcibly dragged down to the beach by increasingly hyperactive kids, they heard the sound of a brass band drawing nearer and nearer. They were about to behold the climax of the week's worldly festivities – a procession down the main street to the strains of the 'Cornish Floral Dance'.

As the band 'oompahed' its merry way towards the place where the intrepid saints were praying and praising, one lady felt an irresistible urge to 'witness' to the musicians. Grabbing a handful of tracts, she ran out of the room, through the dancing throng of revellers and into the midst of the players where she found herself confronted with a major problem. Brass bandsmen, for the most part, need two hands to play! How was she to give them the word? Her hesitation was only momentary. She nimbly wove her way through the marchers, popping a tract daintily into the bell of each instrument.

The second story concerns a friend of mine, Norman Barnes. On the basis of the pressure to witness, in his young days as a pastor, Norman called his church to evangelise. They identified their area as being 6,000 homes and determined that their small group of believers would visit each home three times. That's 18,000 calls! First, they dropped a portion of the Bible through each letter box, then they gave an invitation to the church meetings and finally made a personal call. Hours and hours of work and effort went into the outreach and the sum total of the response was that one person came to the church.

You may be thinking that only eternity will reveal the full impact of what they did. Maybe that is so, though I'm convinced that if you fire a machine gun indiscriminately sooner or later you'll hit someone – but that doesn't make you a marksman. Surely the Holy Spirit can enable us to make better use of our time and resources.

Are these situations really examples of what it means to be a witness? I think not – although I would be loath to write them off altogether as I'm constantly amazed at the things God blesses and uses.

The kingdom here and now

Most evangelicals and charismatics have a limited understanding of what the word 'witness' actually means, which may stem from a superficial application of Acts 1:8: 'You will receive power when the Holy Spirit comes on you; and you will be my witnesses.' One reason for this is that we fail to look at the verse in its context. The disciples had just asked the risen Jesus if he was about to restore the kingdom to Israel. The Lord warned them that it was not for them to concern themselves with times and dates. He went on to explain that they would receive power when the Holy

Spirit came on them and then they would become his witnesses. It's fairly obvious to me that Jesus was not changing the subject but continuing with the same theme – the kingdom. To put it another way, Jesus was saying, 'Don't worry about the fullness of the kingdom and when things are to be wrapped up. I'll give you the Holy Spirit and he will release power in your lives so that you can be witnesses to the kingdom here and now, not only in Jerusalem, Judea and Samaria but to the ends of the earth and to the end of the age for that matter.'

Now, I am not knocking evangelism as a priority. What I hope to get across is that witnessing is much more than telling folk about Jesus, important though that is. I also want to underline the fact that in order to be successful witnesses we need the Holy Spirit and his power, and that power is the power of the coming kingdom. Our message is the gospel of the kingdom which must be preached in the power of the Spirit, with signs following. These signs are the evidence that the kingdom of heaven is at hand. In other words, the Holy Spirit which rested on Jesus is given to us to continue the same ministry which he began, in the same way, with the same power. During his days on earth he was the Witness; now we, the body of Christ, are called to be the witness. Again and again Jesus emphasised his total dependence on the Holy Spirit, and constantly insisted that he could do nothing of himself. Good ideas will not get this job done any more than passively sitting around waiting for revelation as to what to do. We must be actively working in partnership with the Holy Spirit and with one another. We must seek to understand his will and strategy for us as individuals, and as a church.

In this respect we can truly praise God for Billy Graham and the multitudes who have come into the kingdom through his great crusades and consistent witness. But as I stood in the crowds gathered at Earl's Court during the 1989 mission, I was more than ever aware that we have come to the end of an era. Not that great meetings like those are finished, far from it, but such evangelism must include room for Holy Spirit-inspired worship and opportunity to use spiritual gifts, else I fear we shall be moving in disobedience to the Lord. It is time for an even greater manifestation of kingdom life and power as we seek to reach out to those in darkness.

Witnesses to the truth

Now let us look more closely at the word 'witness' and try to appreciate the full meaning of the word. Since the very earliest times the Lord made it a condition that before any judgements could be passed, he required the testimony of at least two witnesses. This was the legal minimum as stated in Deuteronomy 19:15: 'One witness is not enough to convict a man accused of any crime or offence he may have commited. A matter must be established by the testimony of two or three witnesses.' This is the law of God and he has chosen to stand by this in terms of his own final judgement of the world, as we shall see.

There are three elements necessary to make a good witness. First, he must have seen for himself the thing to which he is giving testimony; second, he must be committed to telling the absolute truth without partiality or compromise; third, he must be willing to die for that truth. Without these three qualifications we will not have a very reliable witness. Picking up the third point, we discover something startling about the word witness itself. The Greek word for witness is *martus*, from which we derive our word martyr! In fact, the word grew into its current meaning because so many witnesses had to pay with their lives for the truth which they had seen. Even today, the police will guard an important witness because they realise that his life is very likely to be in danger. In Isaiah 43 the Lord declares to his people, 'You are my witnesses' (vv 10,

12), and at the start of the same chapter promises his protection so that our testimony will not be lost. In order to be a witness in Christian terms, we must agree our three requirements with one other. We must be full of the Holy Spirit.

Let's take a look at Stephen, the very first witness in the early church. His story appears in Acts 7. Here, we see that he fulfils all that is needed to make a trusted Christian witness. He was full of the Holy Spirit – this was a condition of his service as a deacon (Acts 6:3–5), and is confirmed later (Acts 7:55); he saw the resurrected Jesus standing at the right hand of the Father in glory (7:56); he spoke as he saw, holding nothing back; and last, he gave his life for the truth. Personally, I believe that Stephen, being the first witness, was a kind of prototype or example. Multitudes have followed in his footsteps, sacrificing their lives for the truth they held dear. However, the model of Stephen's witness and martyrdom must speak to the whole church as we draw near to the close of this age and as the battle against evil rages stronger yet.

The witness of the church

It is not necessary to go into a detailed study of the Book of Revelation to see that the throne of God and of the Lamb is a central theme. The book starts with the throne (1:4); it promises the faithful a place on the throne (3:21); describes the scene around the throne (4:5), and goes on throughout to focus our attention there. The book draws to a close with judgement from thrones, around which were gathered the souls of the martyr witnesses (20:4). We also see the great white throne, God's ultimate place of judgement (20:11,12). Finally, we hear God's pronouncement from the throne: 'I am making everything new' (21:5), and see that a pure river of life for healing is flowing from that very same place (22:1–2).

For me, the pivotal point of the whole Book of Revelation is chapter 12, where we are introduced to 'a great and wondrous sign'. A woman is pregnant and about to give birth. A dragon, accompanied by a third of the stars (or angels) of heaven, confronts the woman, ready to devour her seed. The baby is born, a man-child set to rule the nations. He is caught up to the throne and miraculously preserved until he is ready to fulfil his destiny in battle. We see here a picture which has been close to God's heart from the beginning of time: a woman, or virgin, conceiving and giving birth to a saviour-child who will bring an end to warfare and suffering by ruling from the throne. This promise was first given to Eve in the Garden of Eden. It was confirmed by the prophets and came to reality through Mary and Jesus. But I believe this particular passage is not referring to Mary and Jesus; they have already played their parts. It is pointing us to some other fulfilment of God's design. We must find another explanation which holds to the essential ingredients of the vision and is in harmony with the rest of Scripture.

Every work or movement of the Holy Spirit is initiated to give birth to Jesus in the lives of God's people and in the body of Christ. The Spirit's chief concern is always to reveal Jesus in and through us. In every age he looks to his people for a virgin bride upon whom he can rest, as he did upon Mary. Then, in Spirit, Jesus can be born, grow to maturity and be seen to be alive in the church of that generation. There is a sense in which every such move of the Spirit is an enactment of this scenario, and always Satan and his angels are there seeking to destroy the infant, just as they attempted to slay the baby Jesus when he was born 2,000 years ago. However, although there are many wonderful fulfilments of this picture, there will come one supreme fulfilment as we draw near to the end of all things. As Satan waxes more and more powerful and darkness covers the earth, so the glory and light of God will arise upon his people. The Spirit of Jesus will be born out of, and through his church and God will have his witnesses even during that time of unprecedented evil.

As we read on in Revelation 12 we observe that the scene changes in verse 7. The man-child, now caught up to the heavenly throne and thus totally preoccupied with the lordship of Jesus, is in the place of authority. The angels of God are now able to engage the dragon and he is cast down to the earth where he is finally overcome. So, Satan, who was in the heavenly realm with authority, is now earth-bound and defeated, the man-child who was earth-bound and powerless is in heaven with authority. That this passage does not portray Jesus as the man-child can be seen from the plurality of those wonderful, oft quoted words, which follow in verse 11 and underline the glorious truth that we will have a share in the victory Christ has already won. He will not be alone as an overcomer for by his grace we will join him in heaven, not, of course, through our own strength or power, for *they* overcame 'by the blood of the Lamb', 'the word of *their* testimony' and '*they* did not love their lives so much as to shrink from death.' The man-child, or mature church, at last becomes the witness Christ called us to be! Jesus in all his glory is manifest first in his corporate, spiritual, body for all the world to see before he comes in his glorified physical body.

I hold dear, and look forward with great anticipation to Jesus' personal return to earth. Nevertheless, I believe that we have majored so much on his Second Coming that we have neglected to understand and emphasise the importance of his prior mystical coming in his spiritual body, which is the church. We must not be satisfied or rest from our labours until we see this 'fulness of Christ' (Eph. 4:13) is attained within at least a significant minority of the church. We saw in an earlier chapter that the whole creation is eagerly waiting for this revealing of 'the many sons of God', as that event will coincide with the return of 'the one Son of God', who is the Head of the body. It will be the sign that our adoption is complete, and will trigger the redemption of our bodies as the last enemy – death – is overcome.

We have been considering Revelation 12, but the previous chapter throws some fascinating light on the subject of witnesses. In it we see some strong links with Zechariah 4, which we looked at in Chapter 2 above. Chapter 11 opens with John being given a rod and told to measure the Temple and its altar, and also to count the worshippers. The completion of the house, which involves the repairing of the altar and the number of true worshippers, is a vital key to unfolding the church's role at the end of the age. As the prophet Haggai, a contemporary of Zechariah, pointed out, God's house does not get built when we put all our resourses and effort into our own dwellings. It is those who serve and worship at the heavenly altar who, with their devotion and obedience, actually form the spiritual temple which God is looking for today.

John's measuring confirmed that everything in the Temple itself was in order, but still there was much that was evil and unclean within the Temple precincts (11:2). However, enough had been accomplished for the Lord to give power to his 'two witnesses' to 'prophesy for 1,260 days', or three and a half years (11:3). This is equivalent to the period of time from the beginning of Jesus' ministry to his death on the cross. It is also the same amount of time that the woman was cared for in the wilderness and that the man-child ruled with authority from the throne (12:5–6). It is clear to me that there is a definite association between these periods, whether or not we take them as literal time spans. We have established that Jesus is our pattern and that we, his body, are to follow in his footsteps giving testimony and witness, as he did, to the kingdom of God. We too then, as his representatives, will have our '1,260 days' of ministry in word and in the power of the Spirit. We too, his church, will be called to 'love not our lives so much as to shrink from death'.

Jesus, 'the one Son', set the example for us, 'the many sons'. We are to live as he lived, love as he loved, die as he died and rise as he rose, in order that a full and complete testimony may be given. That testimony must first be given to the world so that they may see a true witness to the Father's love and power. But it must also be given to the Father that he may judge the fullness of evil which is brought into the open by the reaction of those wicked men who, under the influence of the Beast, reject and slay God's witnesses (11:7). The two witnesses are identified, by the miracles they performed, with all God's other witnesses from the beginning of time. Prophets pointed to the testimony of Jesus and his church, and many paid with their lives for the message they bore. In particular, Moses and Elijah, who appeared with Jesus on the mount of transfiguration, are singled out by inference (11:6) as the two great witnesses of the Old Covenant, representing the Law and the Prophets. Both performed miracles which attested their authority and both were utterly rejected by the worldly rulers of their day. They were types or shadows of the two witnesses yet to come.

So the two witnesses of Revelation 11 are also the man-child of Revelation 12, and both are pictures of the church of Jesus in the last days. The two witnesses are the one many-membered body of Christ. This is confirmed by the difficulty the Bible translators have with verse 8 of chapter 11, which should literally read, 'Their (plural) dead body (singular) will lie in the street' – two witnesses finally slain for their testimony, but only one body! Revelation 12 actually picks up the story of chapter 11 and gives us a different perspective. Whereas chapter 11 looks at things from an earthly aspect, chapter 12 shows us events from a heavenly point of view. Some insist that chapter 12 is a chronological progression from chapter 11: certainly the literal resurrection does finally enable the church to occupy the throne and achieve her ultimate victory. Nevertheless, I also believe that we must see them as parallel, as the church must obtain the authority of the throne in order to gain victory and resurrection. So once more we find that the throne is both starting place and objective.

But there is another important link back to Zechariah 4 which I must refer to before concluding this section. These witnesses 'are the two olive trees and the two lampstands that stand before the Lord of the earth' (11:4). These words echo, almost exactly, the final verse of our Zechariah passage. Here are the olive trees and the lampstands once again, they are placed together and must never be separated. Lampstands, as we have already seen, are symbols of the churches, and the olive trees symbolise the work of the Holy Spirit. The use of these two symbols shows us that the work of the church cannot survive if it is separated from the Holy Spirit. The fact that there are only two candlesticks here, when seven are mentioned in chapter 1, should serve as an additional reminder that only those lamps which are trimmed and lit will fulfil the role of witnesses. Again, here is our significant portion, two-sevenths of the whole church. Other renderings for 'the two who are anointed' (Zech 4:14) are 'sons of fresh oil' or 'shining ones'. It is impossible to overstate the importance of the work of the Holy Spirit through a mature shining church to accomplish God's purposes as history moves to its climax. We are called to be the light of the world. Individually and corporately we must be saturated by a fresh outpouring or anointing of the Holy Spirit if we are to meet this description. We cannot achieve the objectives of pulling down strongholds and setting free those who are in prison without him whom the Father sent to empower us. The angel's words to Zecharaiah must be kept constantly before us: 'Not by might, nor by power, but by my Spirit....'

Sound sermons and good preaching are not enough. We are called to prophesy and to act out and, possibly, to die for the message under the unction of the Third Person of the Trinity. Only then will the gospel of the Kingdom impact all the nations and every single people group represented on earth. Only then will we scale the high walls of false religion, materialism and secularism, bringing down their fortresses. Only then will the Jew be provoked to jealousy, as he sees the Gentile church enjoying the benefits and powers of a kingdom which he considers to be rightfully his.

Surely this puts witnessing on an altogether different plane. Let's not cease gossiping the good news and sharing Jesus at a very personal level. Let's not stop our local church efforts to reach the areas where we live and work, or even our national strategies – may the Lord richly bless them all. But at the same time let us pray fervently that the tide of life in the Spirit will continue to rise in the worldwide church daily, until the glory of God is seen to flood out from us. Let us prevail until there can be no more doubt that Jesus is alive, because he is clearly visible everywhere among his people in character and power. Then we can expect all hell to be let loose as Satan seeks to destroy this manifestation and embodiment of Jesus in our lives. Then we shall understand the full meaning and receive the comfort of our Lord's amazing promise, 'Surely I am with you always, to the very end of the age.'

15

Grandma's promise box

John

Promise boxes have gone out of fashion these days, apparently replaced by tear-off calendars with texts. These latter usually find their way into the 'smallest room' in the house. Perhaps this is because we Christians need something spiritual to do so that we don't waste any of our precious time, or maybe it's an association of ideas and we've subconsciously linked them with the other tear-off sheets we find there. I expect one day some bright enterpreneur will combine the two and invent inspirational loo paper with a different verse for each sheet, colour-coded with different themes.

In Grandma's day it was promise boxes that were in vogue. For the uninitiated, a promise box is a postcard-sized box with a hinged lid which, when opened, reveals dozens of rolled-up pieces of paper packed together like tiny scrolls. The box usually contains a pair of tweezers which enables one to neatly select a curl of paper. On the miniature sheet is written a promise from the word of God. I guess our Chinese friends would view them rather like a kind of Christian fortune cookie. For me, I look back on it more as spiritual bingo, as we wondered who would get the jackpot or promise of the day! Others used promise boxes rather like the world uses horoscopes, hoping that the 'promise' would bring light, guidance or blessing on the day's happenings. Certainly Grandma, who kept the box in the sideboard with the condiments, would often produce it at breakfast or as friends were leaving after a visit. It saved reading long passages of the Bible and left us feeling we'd done the spiritual bit.

The scene was almost always the same. The less spiritual visitors or members of the family invariably felt obliged to take part and feigned interest to cover their embarrassment. The rest put on their polite 'spiritual' voices and 'oohed' and 'aahed' as each wonderful verse was drawn from the box. The whole procedure oozed sentiment, although at times the Lord unashamedly blessed someone.

One-sided truth

'I will never leave you', 'Underneath are the everlasting arms', 'I am the Lord that healeth thee', 'For God so loved the world...' – one after another the promises rolled and the box never let us down. Only years later did I discover why, as a simple child, I was not greatly blessed. Our particular box was pure concentrated sugar; all the valuable nutrients had been removed. It was all blessing and no correction and as such had lost its power to build us up.

Never once do I remember hearing, 'Judgement begins at the house of the Lord', 'I will spew thee out of my mouth', 'Weep and howl for your miseries that will come upon you', and so on. (For obvious reasons, this diet would not go down well at a family breakfast.) God appeared to me to be too good to be true and Christianity was nice, even wonderful, but it didn't really seem to work. This may be why I ended up backsliding for so many years. It was much later in life, as I began to seek God afresh after discovering the devil to be personal and powerful, that I found the Lord to be as devastatingly honest as he was gracious, and for me this put his love in a totally new light. I saw that God is not a Father who only encourages and never rebukes, but that his rebuke is actually part of his love. I also saw that he does not try to pull the wool over my eyes with sentiment, pretending that the path to heaven is strewn with roses. No, he tells it like it is, and I began to learn to take the rougher promises with the smooth. Looking back, I don't know why Grandma got us into this concept, because she was a lady whose faith had seen many trials and testings and came through as gold. She constantly triumphed in adversity, proving God's promises to be true over and over again.

The good and the bad

I believe that the Holy Spirit is seeking a new breed of saint: saints who have learned to receive correction without feeling that God has let them down or that he is unfair: saints who accept that they're in warfare and that there will be hardships; and saints who also know that they're not alone, there's someone in the fire with them. Another promise which I don't remember seeing in Grandma's box, but which I find myself thinking of again and again when meditating on our role as we engage in the final battle, is found in 2 Timothy 3:12. Paul was talking about his own sufferings when suddenly he interjects with these words: 'In fact, everyone who wants to live a godly life in Christ Jesus will be persecuted.' This 'promise' is confirmed elsewhere in Scripture and therefore, although I don't wish to become morbid or appear to welcome suffering, I want us to face the reality of it and understand what's happening when it comes, otherwise we may be found to be in confusion and depression or even working against the Holy Spirit.

Suffering is a subject most of us try to avoid. There is an extreme school of thought in the church that would have us believe that if we are truly 'in faith', suffering should play no part at all in the life of the Christian; all should be triumph and prosperity. This emphasis tends to draw its adherents from the richer nations, although not entirely. The opposite view is equally unbalanced. For some poverty is almost a virtue in itself, and they feel guilty if they succeed in any way, especially financially.

Jamie Buckingham, an American charismatic known for his writing, put things into perspective when he spoke at one of our spring conferences in Brentwood, Essex. 'I believe,' he said, with a cheeky grin playing around the corners of his mouth, 'that our God will prosper us to the extent that we will lack nothing that we need to do the work he has called us to do!' I guess that's just about where I stand. Constantly I ask the Lord to increase my ability to request greater things, both in terms of opportunities and resources.

However, any emphasis that eliminates suffering completely from its teaching is deficient and will finally lead us into deception or disillusionment. Of course, God does not plan how we might suffer. His design in Christ is to eradicate all manner of hardship and pain totally. Nonetheless, while Satan continues to be with us, and while man has the freedom to choose to do good or evil, suffering will remain part of our experience. The remarkable thing is that God uses everything that is turned over to him, even suffering.

Counted worthy to suffer

At this juncture I need to differentiate between two forms of suffering. There is the suffering which every human being experiences to a lesser or greater degree, simply because we're in this world. This may be physical, material or emotional pressure which comes upon us through circumstances or relationships and is unrelated, at least directly, to our being Christians. Often people in the world cope with these kind of difficulties better than we, who claim to be the Lord's, and this is sad because it weakens our testimony. Then there is suffering for the gospel's sake, or persecution, which comes as a direct result of our obedience to the call of Christ and our response to the Holy Spirit. This form of hardship is usually related to our godliness, and not all are considered worthy of this privilege, as we see from Acts 5:41: 'The apostles left the Sanhedrin [having been flogged for their witness], rejoicing because they had been counted worthy of suffering disgrace for the Name [of Jesus].'

Folk responding to the gospel in the early church came into the church understanding, even expecting, that things would not be easy. They realised that they were at the centre of the conflict between the kingdom of light and the powers of darkness. Jesus laid this on the line on a number of occasions. It is he who said, 'Deny yourself, take up your cross and follow me', 'Whoever loses his life for my sake will find it', 'Blessed are those who are persecuted because of righteousness', 'When you are persecuted in one place, flee to another', 'Do not be afraid of those who kill the body', and I could go on. In fact, it appears that Jesus made it quite difficult for people to get involved with him as he openly promised trials, alongside the assurance of rewards. Often we make it easy for people to come into the kingdom, overemphasising the blessings and underplaying the cost. Then we wonder why they are miserable and half-hearted, always moaning about the price they have to pay as disciples of Jesus.

Not only do we complain wrongly, but we also confuse suffering for the gospel with the regular problems of life. When Jesus spoke about 'our cross', he was talking about something we take up voluntarily. He was not referring to those events which come along regardless of our response to him. Those things are not the cross. Just as some people mistakenly blame the devil for things for which they themselves are responsible, so others blame the cross for every hardship life brings along. If the car breaks down it's 'the cross', if it rains it's 'the cross', and so on. This attitude produces a martyr complex, gives a false impression of holiness and makes you miserable into the bargain.

One particular group I heard about years ago were heavily into 'the cross'. When they met and asked one another, 'How are you?' invariably the answer, given with furrowed brow, was, 'Going through, brother, going through.' I'm told one chap met a sister on the way to the meeting and enquired as to her welfare. Receiving the familiar answer, 'Going through, going through,' he ventured further to ask what the problems were. 'Well, dear brother,' she replied, 'as I was getting ready for the meeting this morning, first of all the elastic in my suspender belt snapped and then – then,' she cried, her voice reaching a crescendo, 'the milk boiled over! It's all the cross and I'm going through.' If that's the cross I'll eat my copy of the *UK Christian Handbook*! Why, the average person in the world struggling to survive endures more suffering of that order in a day than many sheltered saints do in a month of Sabbaths.

No, the cross has to be related to persecution which comes in connection with our choice to follow in Christ's footsteps and be led by the Holy Spirit. The cross, in its foolishness, identifies us with Christ in his suffering and releases his resurrection in our lives. Thus we become like him in maturity and in ability, in character and in power. The tragedy is that we have not allowed the Holy Spirit to work out the full effects of the cross in us. We remain immature and such power as we have can be terribly misused. In this respect Samson, as a type of the church, has much to teach us both by way of warning and encouragement.

The ultimate triumph

Samson was one of my favourite Bible characters as a boy. His bravado and strength appealed to me and I loved the way he taunted and despised Israel's enemies, often defeating them single-handed. With his bare hands he slew the lion, and with only the jaw bone of an ass he slaughtered a thousand men. He ripped up city gates and broke ropes as if they were thread. But he was vulnerable, and the Philistines found a way through his defences. His maturity and morals did not match his power, and finally he fell foul of both.

This account should be of particular relevance to Western Christian leaders, especially those who are being used in the power gifts. How easy it is for us to put our heroes on a pedestal and set them up for a fall. I believe we need to discover what Paul meant in 1 Corinthians 12:28. He wrote these words to a church who 'came behind in no spiritual gift', yet whose moral stability was very much in question: 'In the church God has appointed first of all apostles, second prophets, third teachers, then workers of miracles, also those having gifts of healing....'

Powerful gifts do not in themselves equip a man or woman to become an expert in all matters. Our awareness of a lack of power sometimes leaves us open and gullible in the face of success in that area. We feel that we have no right to question the one whom God uses in this way. Of course, there's a difference between cynicism, or unbelief, and genuine pastoral concern. There are a number of books circulating at present which manage to find fault with all those at the forefront of renewal. That's not what I'm talking about. God has instituted an order in the church for our security; miracles and healings are listed after 'first of all apostles, second prophets, third teachers'. All of these ministries should be deeply concerned about the quality and character of our lives, as their first call is to make disciples who follow Jesus in everything that he commanded (Mt 28:19). We must learn to keep rank and to protect one another; otherwise, like Samson, we will find ourselves in serious trouble.

Due to his folly, the Philistines overcame Samson. The Spirit withdrew his strength and he was left powerless, like any other man. Soon he found himself not only in chains with his eyes gouged out, but doing the work of an animal as he trod out corn for his captors. How often throughout history has the church found herself in just this position? Because of her indiscretion she becomes weak, with nothing to distinguish her from false religions. Chained, and without spiritual sight, she actually gives grist to Satan's mill, stockpiling sustenance for her enemies through her hypocrisy and shame. Even now we hear words of condemnation from the world: 'If that's supposed to be Christianity, we want nothing to do with it!' But right here, when all seems lost and hopeless, we see a most remarkable happening which demonstrates the amazing grace of God, the kind of grace we see even more clearly in Jesus who said to weak men whom he knew would miserably fail him, 'I will never leave you!'

Although God's power deserted Samson, his Comforter did not. Right in the bowels of hell itself the Spirit wooed the sinner and God's goodness led Samson to repentance. For those who feel they are so far outside the will of God that he can never use them again, here is a wonderful message of hope. The minute we turn to God in humility and true repentance we will find ourselves in the very place where he can use us best! This is a mystery which we will never understand. Once Samson had yielded to God in total weakness, he was in the most effective place he could possibly be to do his enemies fatal damage. He found himself in the centre of God's will.

There, in the temple of Dagon, he was at the very heart of the Philistine's powerhouse. The enemies of God actually brought him into their stronghold themselves, assured that they had won the final victory. But now, at the eleventh hour, Samson's character had come into line with his power and he gave himself to the Lord as a living sacrifice. In one last, great act of obedience he slew more Philistines than in the whole of the rest of his life, and in the same moment pulled down the pillars on which all the Philistine authority and structure rested. Let this increase our faith and encourage us to believe that the church of Jesus Christ will ultimately triumph over Satan, even though he brings us to the very brink of failure. Jesus' words ring in our ears as being as true as when he first spoke them 2,000 years ago: 'I will never leave you', 'I will build my church…the gates of Hades will not overcome it.'

The church has looked in pretty bad shape, and still does in many places, but repentance is a tremendous thing. In Revelation 3:20 we hear the wonderful invitation of Christ which we apply, often with great success, to the wayward sinner: 'Here I am! I stand at the door and knock. If anyone hears my voice and opens the door, I will go in and eat with him, and he with me.' The offer is, in fact, made to a backslidden church, which, in arrogance and pride, has shut its Lord and Master out. He has not left this church, but patiently waits outside, knocking and looking for a way back in. The exciting thing is that if we open the door to the throne room of our lives, he will open the door to his heavenly throne room: 'To him who overcomes, I will give the right to sit with me on my throne,' Jesus cried (Rev 3:21). Immediately, John declares, 'After this I looked, and there before me was a door standing open in heaven' (Rev 4:1). Suddenly he was in the throne room of God.

All individuals or churches who open their doors to enthrone Jesus as Lord will find that God opens heaven's doors to them and exalts them to a place of trusted authority. Like Samson of old and the man-child of the end-time, we will find that the throne is available to those who will offer themselves sacrificially – body, soul and spirit – to God for his purposes. You see, power is not a problem to

God; it is not something he is short of. What God does lack
is men and women who can be trusted with his power. He
is looking for those who, like Jesus, the Captain of our salvation, have been made perfect through suffering. Perfection, or better, maturity, tends not to grow alongside
power and blessing, but is refined in the fires of spiritual
tribulation and opposition, just as gold is purified through
natural fire.

Authority and power

John the Baptist promised that Jesus would baptise us with
the Holy Spirit and with fire. Fire descended on the Day of
Pentecost to purify the church as well as to empower, and
wherever the Holy Spirit is moving in any measure, the fire
will not be far away. Surrendering and going through the
purifying fire now is our insurance that the fire of judgement which is to come will not consume us on that day. So
the work of the fire is twofold: first, to purify us and to
reveal Christ's character in us, and second, to enable us by
imparting Christ's gifts to us.

There are two Greek words which describe the power of
the Spirit seen in the church: *exousia* and *dunamis*. Just as
there were two olive trees in Zechariah 4, but one oil, so
we recognise that there are two aspects of the Spirit's work
among the Lord's people, but only one Spirit. *Exousia*
refers to the power which accompanies privilege and delegated authority on the basis of character, and *dunamis*,
means ability and is, in my mind, linked with the response
of faith. The first kind of power relates to the fruit of the
Spirit, the second to the gifts of the Spirit; both are absolutely necessary if a full testimony to Jesus is to be seen
through the church in all the earth. Here again are our two
witnesses: the witness of Jesus' character and the witness of
his power. Both must be visible for all men, everywhere, so
they can observe the fullness of Christ's authority seen in

the Lamb and the Lion, those apocalyptic symbols of his character and power.

Sadly, the church in its divisions falls into the trap of recognising one or other of these emphases. We are either fruit fads or power crazy and tend to despise those at the other end of the spectrum from ourselves. Unfortunately, one witness is not sufficient and so our testimony goes largely unheeded. Fruit and gifts, character and power, suffering and abounding must go together, and it is the Holy Spirit who makes this a reality.

In conclusion, let the words of two great apostles, who themselves experienced tremendous suffering for the sake of the gospel, speak their own encouragement:

Therefore, since Christ suffered in his body, arm yourselves also with the same attitude, because he who has suffered in his body is done with sin. As a result, he does not live the rest of his earthly life for evil human desires (1 Pet 4:1–2).

Dear friends, do not be surprised at the painful trial you are suffering, as though something strange were happening to you. But rejoice that you participate in the sufferings of Christ, so that you may be overjoyed when his glory is revealed (1 Pet 4:12–13).

Consider it pure joy, my brothers, whenever you face trials of many kinds, because you know that the testing of your faith develops perseverance. Perseverance must finish its work so that you may be mature and complete, not lacking anything (Jas 1:2).

In this you greatly rejoice, though now for a little while you may have had to suffer grief in all kinds of trials. These have come so that your faith – of greater worth than gold, which perishes even though refined by fire – may be proved genuine and may result in praise, glory and honour when Jesus Christ is revealed (1 Pet 1:6–7).

16

Our feet shall stand...

John

The lads were off to take the usual Saturday night open-air meeting in Soho, in London's West End, but I declined to go on this occasion. I wanted to study and prepare for the meeting I was taking the next day. There was some good-natured ribbing going on as Richard and I loaded the speaker's stand into the back of the van. They obviously wanted me to change my mind and go with them, so they piled on the condemnation, but my mind was made up. Eventually, I waved goodbye as the van accelerated away with its enthusiastic and determined crew. I sat down at my desk relieved that I had managed to stand my ground and excited that I had found some time to get down to the word.

The guarantee of victory

I'd been thinking quite a bit about Nebuchadnezzar's dream and was intrigued by the interpretation Daniel gave of its meaning (Dan 2:31–45). The king had seen a huge and impressive statue with a head of gold, chest and arms of silver, belly and thighs of bronze, legs of iron, and feet, part iron and part clay. The image represented the kingdoms from that moment until 'the God of heaven will set up a kingdom that will never be destroyed'. I took a large sheet of paper and began to draw my idea of what I thought the statue must have looked like. I coloured each section in and neatly wrote the names of the kingdoms alongside. I was clear about the head of gold, that was Babylon, the silver chest with its two arms represented the Medes and Persians, the bronze belly and thighs the Greek Empire under Alexander the Great and the iron was obviously the Roman Empire. After that I got a bit vague. I didn't really like the thought that ten European nations would link together like ten toes and combine the forces of the Roman Empire and Communism, represented by the iron and clay. But I knew that if we were in the days when the feet kingdoms of the image were about to be revealed, then the rock cut out from the mountain must also be about to do its work of crushing those evil kingdoms to a powder (Dan 2:42, 45).

The time had fled by and it was getting on for 1 am in the morning. Everyone in the house had gone to bed and the street outside was quiet. I had no idea of the hour, I was so taken up with my thoughts. My heart was pounding with excitement as I realised how near to the end of all things we must be. There was much to be done and the return of Jesus to this planet could be very soon. Then the front doorbell shattered the silence and I almost leaped right out of my skin with fear! Who on earth – if indeed they were from the earth – could it be at this hour of the night? I cautiously crept out of my study to check the front door, only to be stopped dead in my tracks. There, through the rippled glass, I could just make out a massive shape and a head which peered menacingly at me through the upper light of the front door. The creature was all of seven feet six inches tall and all I could think of was the image which had been staring back at me from my desk for the last few hours.

As I stood glued to the spot, the bell rang again, signalling impatience. My only option was to open the door as the monster would easily break it down anyway if I refused. With trembling hand I turned the lock and gingerly opened up. "Ello mate, what took you so long then?' the monster enquired. I looked up into the smiling face of Richard, who was perched on top of the speaker's stand which he had decided to return as my study light was still burning. 'Thanks a million,' I replied. 'Do you realise I nearly died of fright?' 'Wouldn't be any great loss,' he said encouragingly as he lugged the stand into the hall and went on his way.

Ever since that evening, the picture of Nebuchadnezzar's image has been engraved in my mind! When I eventually got back to my studies I began to realise something even more significant. Although the kingdoms represented by the image existed in their varying degrees of glory in history, each one is now also revealed in a spiritual and abstract way in the world today. The statue now stands in all its enormity, brilliance and accumulated evil, with its feet firmly planted on the earth which is rightfully ours in Christ. For example, Satan controls the world through wealth, Babylon, the materialistic head of gold, is with us, as are all the other subservient powers which together dominate the earth and demand that everyone bows down to worship the image. However, in the invisible, heavenly realm, Christ the Rock, cut from the mountain without hands, has already dealt a fatal blow to this devilish structure through his death and resurrection. Now we, the church, fashioned in his likeness, must follow suit in the visible, earthly realm, and claim what is ours. Like Peter, we are 'little rocks' or 'living stones', also made without hands by the creative power of the

Holy Spirit, through whom we too have authority to grind Satan's earthly strongholds to dust.

If we love and obey the Lord our God, then the assurances made to his people as they prepared to enter and possess the promised land, inhabited by giants, is still applicable today. The church is called to join the heavenly battle which will finally rid the whole earth of satanic influence and put the authority where it truly belongs. Following in the footsteps of Jesus, we too can tread on scorpions and serpents (Luke 10:19) and so claim the land, for 'every place where you set foot shall be yours' (Deut 11:24). Jesus fulfilled the promise made in Genesis 3:15 by placing his heel on Satan's head and crushing him. Now the way is open for us to do the same in his name. When we tread on the enemies who are squatters in this world, and deliver it back to Jesus, he will give it over to us as an inheritance. So our 'feet' play an important part in the reclamation programme.

In contrast to Nebuchadnezzar's vision, John saw a living image, the splendour and power of which put the king's statue into the shade. He saw

> someone 'like a son of man,' dressed in a robe reaching down to his feet and with a golden sash around his chest. His head and hair were white like wool, as white as snow, and his eyes were like blazing fire. His feet were like bronze glowing in a furnace, and his voice was like the sound of rushing waters. In his right hand he held seven stars, and out of his mouth came a sharp double-edged sword. His face was like the sun shining in all its brilliance (Rev 1:13–16).

These two visions are in complete contrast. The one is cold metal, the other is a living body; the one is fixed and silent, the other moves and speaks; the one is fashioned by man's hand, the other has always existed and is alive for ever more! Nebuchadnezzar's statue may offer us a share of its earthly wealth and power for a limited season, but has feet of clay. On the other hand John's figure gives us a place as members in his body for ever and ever. His feet of burning bronze walk in judgement – no wonder John fell there as though dead.

This is the One whose glory is being revealed in the church, the One who is coming with the clouds in splendour with ten thousand of his saints. This is the Christ, the Anointed One, in whom we have an eternal part. He is the Head, we are the arms and shoulders, the belly and thighs, the legs and the feet, and we are called to walk in his judgement as well as in all his other attributes. This is the Christ who has been seen throughout history in differing measure in his church, but who will be plainly visible in his people at the end of the age in all his majesty and power.

Anointed by the Spirit

Psalm 133 confirms, in its typology, Jesus' experiences and his teaching in the New Testament. In this beautiful poem there is a picture of Aaron the priest being anointed with oil. The precious perfumed oil was never to be reproduced or poured upon anyone other than a priest. It was sacred anointing oil (Ex 30:31-33) to be used only as prescribed by the Lord. The oil poured on the head of Aaron ran down his beard without touching his flesh and on to his priestly robes. It was a generous portion, dripping off the fringes of his garments to the floor of the tabernacle and filling the place with its delicate fragrance. So, in his time, Christ our Head and High Priest was anointed with the oil of the Spirit as the Head of the body. He was the first to receive the anointing but soon it ran on to the shoulders and right down to the *feet*. It was a plentiful outpouring but was not given to anoint fleshy appetites and desires, but rather to soak the garments of praise and righteousness which have been provided to cover the body. Still today that oil flows, anointing every priest and member with the aroma of

Christ to walk in his holiness. Sadly, there is much in our renewal movements which is of the flesh and needs to be identified and rejected, but this fact must not hinder us from receiving what is our right in Christ, as his body and royal priesthood.

Actually, the oil of anointing is not the only analogy to the Spirit's blessing in this psalm. It is also likened to the gentle dew which fell on Mount Hermon morning by morning. The oil relates to our call and ministry as priests and is an ordered anointing. Therefore, if we are obedient, we can expect the flow of his blessing to be steady and continuous. The dew, on the other hand, encourages us to believe for the spontaneous, daily blessings which will come as we dwell as God's family in the land he has given us. He will constantly surprise us.

The psalm shows us that brotherly love and dwelling together in unity is a tangible expression of the Spirit's work. It is here that the 'Lord bestows his blessing, even life for evermore'. I believe that these words are prophetic. A moment in history will come when the Lord looks at the oneness of his people and finds that his heart is satisfied. Saints from every country in the world, from every tribe and tongue, will be bound together in practical relationships of love and seen to be one nation under God. It's extremely interesting and relevant to see that in the very next psalm the servants of God are praising him and lifting up holy hands, by night, in the house of the Lord, standing and singing together, not 'please bless me and mine', but 'bless the Lord!'

Satan's final onslaught

Jesus warned, 'Night is coming, when no one can work' (Jn 9:4). In saying this he endorsed Isaiah's prophesy of darkness covering the earth. As that moment approaches, the Lord's servants may be restricted by human and satanic forces in what they are able to do. But no one will be able to stop them standing together as God's house, blessing him through the gloom by unity and peace with one another. They will have ceased from constantly being concerned for themselves and their own welfare, and will be totally preoccupied with the Lord and his satisfaction. It is then that his glory will fill the living temple and shine out as never before. Thus, like her Master, even in apparent defeat the church will be victorious.

Satan is putting all of his powers and resources into obtaining a visible presence on earth, one which will stand in God's place of worship and authority. He intends to dominate the world through a physical throne, proclaiming himself to be God (2 Thess 2:4). If the 'mystery of godliness' (1 Tim 3:16) is that Christ was manifest in the flesh, then the 'mystery of iniquity' (2 Thess 2:7, AV) must surely be that the devil will find himself a body to counterfeit the work of Christ and take away his glory. This Antichrist figure may well be an individual who will stand and occupy the place reserved for Jesus, but Satan will certainly look for an assembly or congregation to live in and to show himself through (Rev 2:9; 3:9). He will deceive and seduce mankind by displaying his material resources and wealth by gathering his lying spirits with their counterfeit signs and wonders. For a brief moment he will enjoy this show of earthly power and the obeisance of men, but his time is strictly limited.

While the Enemy plants his feet on the earth and musters his troops in demonstrations of physical might and supernatural power, Jesus calls his people together in a totally different setting. Zechariah tells us that Jesus' feet will stand on the Mount of Olives (14:4). Some may well argue that this is the literal site of our Lord's return to earth, but even if true there is a spiritual significance which is at least as important. The Mount of Olives is the place to which the Lord calls his church in preparation for his triumphant return. This is the very spot where Jesus prepared to face the cross. It is the place where he prayed, 'Not my will but thine' to his heavenly Father. We have already said that the church will not complete her task of bringing salvation and judgement to the world through displays of human might and power, but from a position of yieldedness and sacrifice. Our path to victory is by way of the Mount of Olives and the cross. In order to receive strength to endure Satan's final acts of violence and hatred against the suffering Christ in us, we must meet with our Jesus in humble submission. Each of us too must pray 'Not my will' as we hand over to the Holy Spirit the right to lead us every step of the way to the very end.

The Garden of Gethsemane, at the foot of the Mount of Olives, was the place of intercession and prevailing prayer without which Jesus would not have had the strength to suffer as he did. This focuses our attention on a vast subject which is beyond the scope of this book, but one which we cannot afford to ignore. Without the fullness of the Holy Spirit the disciples had no sense of urgency; they did not know how to pray, nor did they even have the power to remain awake during our Lord's hour of greatest need. Consequently, while he was able to hold through, they became fearful and confused.

This surely demonstrates to us the absolute necessity of the Holy Spirit's aid in helping us to pray. Jude exhorts us with these words: 'Dear friends, build yourselves up in your most holy faith and pray in the Holy Spirit' (v 20). Paul tells us that 'the Spirit helps us in our weakness. We do not know what we ought to pray, but the Spirit himself intercedes for us with groans that words cannot express' (Rom 8:26). Without the Holy Spirit, prayer becomes a very hit-and-miss affair which will seriously limit our effectiveness. With the Holy Spirit even our sighs and groans take on meaning as he intercedes through us and for us.

If we are the generation through which all things will be

brought to a conclusion (and even if we are not we should live as though we were) we are, in a sense, the feet of the body of Jesus, walking and carrying the church towards that great and final meeting when we shall stand on the Mount with Jesus. By his grace and the enabling of the Holy Spirit we will make it. No satanic or demonic forces will be able to stop us. This step by step progress will not come through any virtue of our own, but through the resurrection Spirit which is at work in us. The resurrection is not God's 'plan B', as it were, to rescue us from failure and final defeat. It is not an unrelated, external answer which the Lord will bring in to rescue us at the end. The resurrection is vitalising us right now. It is the power which changes us from one degree of glory to another. It is a hidden process which is at work, quickening us day by day. It is a kind of metamorphosis which is secretly taking place within us, as in a chrysalis. Soon the butterfly will emerge. Soon we will break out of the limitations of these mortal bodies and receive our heavenly bodies and be complete in Christ. Death, pain, sickness, night, suffering, crying and affliction will have no more effect on us.

Armed for the fight

At the end of Ephesians, the letter which some theologians call 'the church epistle', we are encouraged by Paul to put on the whole armour of God. Because of our individualism, Christians tend to see that as something for each one of us to do personally. But Paul is calling the whole church, as the body of Jesus, to put on the complete set of armour. Each piece speaks of some aspect of Christ himself who is our protection in battle. The belt of truth, the breastplate of righteousness, the shoes of the gospel of peace, the shield of faith, the helmet of salvation and the sword of the Spirit are all vital to our success in warfare. This is not a picture of a few super-keen enthusiasts getting geared up; it is the many-membered church of Jesus standing clothed with Christ 'against the rulers, against the authorities, against the powers of this dark world and against the spiritual forces of evil in the heavenly realms' (Eph 6:12).

Even if we pursue the individual application of each person putting on the whole armour, which is of course justifiable, the armour is made in such a way that it affords the greatest protection when used with the rest of the cohort. For example, when brought together, the shields made what was called a 'turtle' which was almost impenetrable; the breastplate protected only the front and was therefore most effective in a circle.

The wonderful thing is that having done all of this, all we are called to do is 'stand'. Three times in two sentences Paul says 'stand': 'When the day of evil comes...*stand* your ground', 'After you have done everything, *stand*', and '*Stand* firm then' (Eph 6:13–14).

When the children of Israel were trapped between the Egyptian army and the Red Sea, Moses gave the command, '*Stand* still, and see the salvation of the Lord!' (Ex 14:13, AV). The command has not been changed as the church faces being driven into the sea of death by evil principalities and powers. In 2 Thessalonians 2:8 we read that when the 'man of sin' or 'the lawless one' is revealed, 'the Lord Jesus will overthrow [him] with the breath of his mouth and destroy [him] by the splendour of his coming.' Powerful though Satan is, one 'puff' from Jesus will blow him right out of sight. The splendour of Jesus' light banishes darkness. Darkness has no power whatsoever over light. Darkness is merely the absence of light, so when Jesus comes in Person, Satan is no more. That's all there is to it. The battle really is the Lord's, let's get our armour on and stand!

The unfinished task

It would be good to finish a book like this on a note of triumph and victory, but it is better still to come back down to earth where the church's work has yet to be completed. Having been encouraged to see the Holy Spirit's ability to bring us through into the fullness of Christ, we must not forget that there remains a job to be done. The completion of this task of being a living witness to Christ and his kingdom in all the nations of the world determines when the end shall come. God is waiting, Christ is waiting, the nations are waiting. They are waiting for us to go, and the paradox is that only those who are *standing* with there feet shod with the shoes of the gospel of peace can *go*. They are waiting for us to receive the power of the Holy Spirit and respond to the challenge of the world for Christ and of Christ for the world.

Let me leave you with a prophetic word I heard at a Pentecost prayer vigil held in Jerusalem in May 1989. Charismatic leaders from all continents and all denominations gathered to prepare a call to mission to Spirit-filled Christians everywhere. The call is going forth for us to link together in the evangelisation of the world throughout the final decade of this millennium. This is what the Spirit said:

> Today is the time of harvest and ingathering, a time when the Spirit is being poured out upon all flesh in these the last days. It is a time when the vats overflow with wine and oil and the fields are white and heavy for harvest. The Lord, Master of the vineyard, has called forth workers into his vineyard to reap the precious fruit of the earth.
>
> Through the centuries he has called workers into his fields and has promised that they are worthy of their hire. Some have laboured since the third hour, others since the sixth hour, and still others since the ninth hour. These have indeed borne the burden and the heat of the day. And still, the harvest is not finished.
>
> Now, the Lord says, I will send to work at your sides

eleventh-hour workers, those who have been idle because no man would hire them. And, although their work will be short, they will make the difference between success and failure.

Unlike many before them, this army of workers will be mostly young people who will go forth to proclaim the gospel without fear or compromise. Most of their converts will also be young people. They will come from the nations and peoples that you least expect. They are a great company that you do not know at this time, but the Lord is preparing them even now.

They will bring in a harvest that will exceed that of all the other workers combined. Through them, ancient walls and kingdoms will fall. They will be utterly without fear. Through astounding ministries of signs and wonders, many peoples long abandoned and considered unreachable will be brought into the kingdom.

In the end, they will receive the same reward as you who have borne the burden and the heat of the midday sun, even as those who were persecuted and martyred. The day will come when you shall know them and together you will rejoice in the midst of the harvest and in the glorious day of the Lord.

You must pray for and welcome these eleventh-hour workers that I will give to you. You must not be jealous of them but rejoice at the reward that I will give them – for they were willing to come at the last hour – and without them the harvest would not be complete.

The Spirit and the bride say, 'Come!' And let him who hears say, 'Come!' Whoever is thirsty, let him come; and whoever wishes, let him take of the free gift of the water of life (Rev 22:17).

'Amen. Come, Lord Jesus' (Rev 22:20).

APPENDIX

Receiving the Holy Spirit

These notes are not a step-by-step method of receiving the Holy Spirit. They are simply guides and suggestions which may prove beneficial to those who are seeking to be filled, and also to those who wish pray for others to receive the Spirit. Please use them prayerfully and wisely, preferably with assistance from mature Christians known to you, who themselves are baptised in the Holy Spirit. Remember that the primary work of the Spirit is to reveal and glorify Christ in you – his character, power, death and resurrection. New Christians should be encouraged to receive as soon as possible.

There is no reason if you have just become a Christian to wait before receiving the Holy Spirit. You especially need his presence and help, right from the start, and it is very likely that your faith and expectancy are high having recently met with Jesus. Complicated explanations and studies should not be necessary as, in most cases, you will have trust in those who have led you into this new and dynamic relationship with Jesus.

A worshipful context is favourable

The Holy Spirit delights to assist you in your worship of

212

the Lord and it is, therefore, good to be looking outward and upward to God rather than inward. Be active in using your heart, mind and voice to praise the Lord, expressing your love rather than praying and constantly asking him to bless you. Do not be afraid of releasing your emotions to the Spirit; tears, laughter, joy, peace, shouting may well be good and proper – if they come from a right heart they will not be harsh or grating. The Holy Spirit's idea of order and ours are not always compatible.

The laying on of hands may be helpful

The laying on of hands by other Spirit-filled Christians is a perfectly acceptable and scriptural practice in order to receive the Spirit. This should be done prayerfully and not suddenly or without due thought and consideration as the act is a symbolic affirmation. It may also be a point of contact and definite means of imparting blessing, although Jesus is always the One who does the work even if he uses some other agent. Generally, it is wise to lay hands on the head or shoulders and it is usually best to work with others rather than alone to avoid any wrong appearance. Most people receive in this way but it is not an essential ingredient.

The Holy Spirit will not impose himself upon you

The Comforter will not take more than you give him. Unlike Satan and evil spirits, which push, cajole and demand, the Holy Spirit waits until he is invited and never takes the control away from you. You may shake or collapse when the Spirit comes or respond in other unusual ways, but he will not force you to do anything against your will. You are always free to take the helm and can resist the Spirit as well as co-operate with him.

The Spirit has a thousand ways to bless you

Do not get locked into an expectation as to how the Holy Spirit will come to you. One of his great qualities is creativity and within his creation there is tremendous diversity. Be careful not to model your hopes on someone else's experience; this is a trap which has kept many from quickly entering into blessing. Allow the Lord to meet with you in his own special way. Like the patterns in the flames of a fire his presence will be different on every occasion.

Relax and remember that Jesus is the One who baptises you with the Holy Spirit

The Lord may use others as channels or points of contact for you, but Jesus releases the Spirit into your life. Look to him and actively yield to him in the deepest part of your being, as you would surrender yourself to the arms of the one who baptises you in water. Jesus breathed upon his disciples and the breath of God filled them on the Day of Pentecost. It may be helpful for you to relax and breath in gently and deeply. Tension and introversion are positively unhelpful. We have heard of a number of people who were filled with the Holy Spirit as they lay back in the comfort of a warm bath!

It is usually best to pray for people individually

Sometimes people are very conscious of close friends or relatives when they are being prayed for and it may be necessary to separate them. The greater the sense of God's presence in a meeting the less folk are aware of themselves.

Co-operate with the Holy Spirit

We have said that the Spirit will not compel you. It is necessary, therefore, that you work with him. He will not make you laugh, raise your arms or dance; you do not become his puppet. This is especially important in the area of prophesying or speaking out in tongues. The Holy Spirit will not waggle your tongue or operate your vocal chords. You must choose to make the sounds and do the speaking as he gives you the utterance. Do not examine the sounds and words he gives you; they are unintelligible to your mind. If you are looking to Jesus and worshipping, even your groans mean something to him, just as a lover's sigh to the beloved, or a baby's every noise to his mother. Singing out in tongues or prophecy is quite in order and will be a great encouragement to some. Do not wait for a whole sentence in tongues or a whole prophecy to form in your mind. Give what you have received in faith and more will follow if there is more to come.

Feed and exercise your faith

Faith is the key to receiving all the gifts God gives, including the blessing of the Holy Spirit. You, together with every other Christian, have been given a measure of faith which will increase as you hunger and thirst after the Lord and those things he has made available to you. In order to create hunger you need to learn more about God's character and nature as well as his promises. Faith in God, and knowledge of God, come by hearing him speak through his people, through his written word – the Bible – and directly into your heart. So you need to spend time listening to him in each of these ways.

Assure yourself of the scriptural validity of the experience you are seeking

This is particularly important for those who have doubts or have received negative teaching. Read and study, especially the Scriptures, but also other helpful teaching material which will ensure that you are convinced in heart and mind that the baptism of the Holy Spirit is for every believer today. A positive conviction of this truth is essential to fire your faith so that you are able to receive and also continue to walk in God's blessing.

Examine yourself to see if there are any hindrances

Prayerfully and without condemnation ask the Holy Spirit to reveal any blockages there may be in your thinking, will, or emotions. It is possible that there are things from your religious background or your cultural upbringing, such as fear, tradition, rationalism, prejudice, etc, which could seriously impair your faith. Be careful to note that the experience is not for those who have reached perfection or maturity, but for those who seek it. The Spirit comes to help you gain victory over sin – you cannot succeed without the strength he gives. He is not the reward for holy living, but the means by which we live holy lives. He is not the goal, but the gate! Deliberate and unrepented sin which you are determined to indulge in, regardless of a work of the Holy Spirit, will cause him to withdraw and it is very likely that you will feel the negative effects of this in your life in some way.

Expect the devil to oppose the work of the Holy Spirit in your life

Satan and all his minions and forces are dedicated to keeping you from a relationship with the Holy Spirit. They are fully aware that he is your source of strength and that Spirit-filled Christians, living in holiness and power, are their worst enemies. So be prepared for opposition to your receiving the Spirit and to your walking in his blessing and guidance. The Enemy will first seek to work within you, creating doubts and fears in your own mind and, if he is unsuccessful here, he will move outside, sending antagonism from others, sometimes even from our Christian friends. A most common tactic he employs, which snatches away our blessing, is to make us question the gifts we have been given. He will almost certainly tell you that your 'tongue' is made-up gibberish. The best way to combat this is to exercise your 'tongue', or indeed any other gifts or blessings received, in active and open warfare against him. Do not let him get even a toe-hold; make it clear that you mean business from the very start. A word of warning and encouragement in this respect: don't give Satan glory by concentrating on him; we need to be aware of his activities but not to focus on them. Remember that the power of Jesus at work within us is not to be compared to the devil's power – it's the difference between a firecracker and a thermonuclear explosion!

Expect God to move on congregations

Although we have said that it is usually best to pray for people individually, in the Scripture and in revival God moves on whole gatherings. Let us pray for, and begin to expect this, as a corporate experience of the Holy Spirit knits people together as nothing else can. Such experiences will be more and more relevant as we function together in warfare, evangelism and prayer.

Finally, keep the flame burning

There is no reason why your experience should grow dim. The Lord has promised to be with you always, right to the end. He has no lack of resources or heart to walk and work with you. However, you do need to keep close to him and not allow the distractions and cares of this life to draw you away from your link – in the Spirit – to his grace and blessing, of which there is an endless and bountiful supply. If it is your desire to go on with Jesus there is nothing in this world or the next which can keep you back. Hear the words of Paul in Romans 8:35–39:

> Who shall separate us from the love of Christ? Shall trouble or hardship or persecution or famine or nakedness or danger or sword? As it is written: 'For your sake we face death all day long; we are considered as sheep to be slaughtered.' No, in all these things we are more than conquerors through him who loved us. For I am convinced that neither death nor life, neither angels nor demons, neither the present nor the future, nor any powers, neither height nor depth, nor anything else in all creation, will be able to separate us from the love of God that is in Christ Jesus our Lord.

Thou Christ of burning, cleansing flame,
Send the fire!
Thy blood-bought gift today we claim,
Send the fire!
Look down and see this waiting host,
Give us the promised Holy Ghost,
We want another Pentecost,
Send the fire!

God of Elijah, hear our cry:
Send the fire!
To make us fit to live or die,
Send the fire!
To burn up every trace of sin,
To bring the light and glory in,
The revolution now begin,
Send the fire!

'Tis fire we want, for fire we plead,
Send the fire!
The fire will meet our every need,
Send the fire!
For strength to ever do the right,
For grace to conquer in the fight,
For power to walk the world in white,
Send the fire!

To make our weak hearts strong and brave,
Send the fire!
To live a dying world to save,
Send the fire!
O see us on thy altar lay
Our lives, our all, this very day,
To crown the offering now we pray,
Send the fire!

William Booth – Founder of the Salvation Army

The Occult And Young People

by Roger Ellis

Witches, horoscopes, ouija boards, reincarnation...

Day by day our senses are bombarded by occult propaganda; books on spiritism, newspaper reports on the paranormal, horoscopes on the radio, while New Age is all the rage.

This book warns of the dangers of dabbling with forces beyond our control. It also shows a way out for those who have been spiritually and emotionally wounded by demonic powers.

Roger Ellis lays the groundwork for a biblical understanding of the occult and the supernatural, as well as showing us how to take a positive Christian stand in spiritual warfare.

Roger Ellis is based at the Revelation Christian Fellowship in Sussex. He is a member of the Pioneer Team, and has been a regular speaker at Spring Harvest.

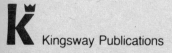
Kingsway Publications

Praying Together

by Mike & Katey Morris

We can all pray on our own. We can know the power of praying with other Christians too.

But what about praying with our marriage partner? Why is it such a problem? Can prayer be fun? Can we worship at home?

If you have ever asked one of these questions, and if you long for greater spiritual unity with your husband or wife, then this book is for you.

This is not a lecture on 'why you should pray more', but a personal and practical manual that will spur you on to action, so that prayer with your partner becomes a living reality, not just some hopeless ideal.

Mike Morris is the Research and Development Officer at the Evangelical Alliance and **Katey** is a secondary school teacher. The seminars that they have led at various Bible-week conventions have shown the enormous need for their practical and spiritual teaching.

Kingsway Publications

Kingsway Publications

Kingsway Publications publishes books to encourage spiritual values in the home, church and society. The list includes Bibles, popular paperbacks, more specialist volumes, booklets, and a range of children's fiction.

Kingsway Publications is owned by The Servant Trust, a Christian charity run by representatives of the evangelical church in Britain, committed to serving God in publishing and music.

For further information on the Trust, including details of how you may be able to support its work, please write to:

> The Secretary
> The Servant Trust
> 1 St Anne's Road
> Eastbourne
> East Sussex BN21 3UN
> England